The Historic
Unfullfilled Promise

The Historic Unfullfilled Promise

HOWARD ZINN

Introduction by Matthew Rothschild

Open Media Series
City Lights Books • San Francisco

Library of Congress Cataloging-in-Publication Data
Zinn, Howard, 1922-2010.
 The historic unfullfilled promise / Howard Zinn ; introduction by
Matthew Rothschild.
    p. cm.
Zinn's feature articles penned for the *Progressive* from 1980 to
2009.
 Includes index.
 ISBN 978-0-87286-555-6
1. United States—History—1969- 2. United States—Foreign
relations—1981-1989. 3. United States—Foreign relations—1989-
4. United States—Politics and government—1981-1989.
5. United States—Politics and government—1989- 6. World
politics—20th century. I. Title.

 E876.Z56 2012
 973.924—dc23

                            2012007955

City Lights Books are published at the City Lights Bookstore
261 Columbus Avenue, San Francisco, CA 94133
www.citylights.com

CONTENTS

INTRODUCTION

By Matthew Rothschild

You're in for a real treat.

This collection of Howard Zinn's work for *The Progressive* contains more wisdom and insight and vision and hope than you'd be able to find almost anywhere else in a book this size.

As you'll see, there is nothing intimidating about his writing. He didn't gussy it up with $100 words or incomprehensible constructions. He wrote not to show off but to communicate to as many people as possible.

The words are not challenging, but the concepts are, in the best sense, because he challenged us to examine the precooked meals we're fed every day as Americans about our identity as a nation, about the necessity of war, about the desirability of capitalism. And he challenged us not only to imagine a more humane, peaceful, democratic, and just society, but also to work toward that goal with persistence and joy.

Some advice at the outset: Get out your yellow highlighter or your red pen because you'll feel the irresistible urge to mark line after line, paragraph after paragraph.

He had a knack for aphorism: For instance, "War is itself the most extreme form of terrorism," and "In between war and passivity, there are a thousand possibilities."

7

And he had a sly sense of humor, which would also come out in his talks and in his personal interactions. You can detect his characteristic wit in his first essay here, where he ridiculed Boston University for kicking Students for a Democratic Society off campus for being violent while allowing the Marines to continue to recruit there since, as Zinn wrote, "the Marine Corps had a well-known record for pacifism."

Or take this opening from "Artists of Resistance": "Whenever I become discouraged (which is on alternate Tuesdays, between three and four)."

He could be very self-effacing. When he'd e-mail these columns in, he'd often write something like, "You don't need to publish it if you don't think it's any good." And when we did the most minor editing (he didn't need much), he would thank us for doing more than we did.

Which reminds me of the time I was interviewing him on *Progressive Radio* about his memoir *You Can't Be Neutral on a Moving Train*. As I recall, I said, "I'm surprised you're so humble, or at least you fake it real well," and he laughed, and said, "Is that a compliment?"

He was a lovable leftist. He took the extra time, even in e-mails, to try to say something considerate. And he liked simple pleasures. After he spoke to a huge crowd in Madison one time, it was getting late, so I asked him if he wanted to go get a drink. "No, but what I'd really like is a milkshake," he said. So we went down the block and had one (I think he ordered a malt), and while we were there he gladly gave a few autographs to people who came up to him.

His wit and graciousness went hand in hand with a profundity that speaks to us today, loudly and clearly, and will serve as a clarion call for generations going forward.

For he was a teacher, above all.

He taught his students at Boston University and his readers all over the world how to study history, how to examine power, how to think radically—and how to resist.

In the very first essay in this collection, he wrote about the need to "move toward the ideals of egalitarianism, community, and self-determination," which he called "the historic, unfulfilled promise of the word *democracy*."

His commitment to egalitarianism comes through in the great interview he did with David Barsamian: "If I had to say what is at the center of left values," Zinn explained, "it's the idea that everyone has a fundamental right to the good things in life, to the necessary things of life, that there should be no disproportions in the world." And then he made it real by adding: "It doesn't mean perfect equality; we can't possibly achieve that. I notice that your sweater is better than mine. But we both have a sweater, which is something."

This egalitarianism underlies his internationalism. He insisted, as he told Barsamian, that "the lives of children in other countries are equivalent to the lives of children in our country." And note the next sentence: "Then war is impossible." Because of his experience as a bombardier in World War II, he knew to the depths of his soul that war murders innocent people, including children, and that the only way people tolerate war is by dehumanizing the victims.

Zinn refused to dehumanize any and all of war's victims. In "Our Job Is a Simple One: Stop Them," he did not exempt even enemy soldiers. "I don't want to insist on the distinction—and this is something to think about—between innocent civilians and soldiers who are innocent."

He invoked as evidence the notorious Turkey Shoot in the first Gulf War when the U.S. military mowed down Saddam Hussein's conscripts, who were in full retreat.

Zinn understood that soldiers give their lives not for some noble purpose but because of the actions of power-crazed leaders. U.S. soldiers who died in the Iraq War "did not die for their country," he wrote. "They died for their government. They died for Bush and Cheney and Rumsfeld. And yes, they died for the greed of the oil cartels, for the expansion of the American empire, for the political ambitions of the president. They died to cover up the theft of the nation's wealth to pay for the machines of death."

So he asked, in "After the War": "Should we begin to think, even before this shameful war is over, about ending our addiction to massive violence and instead using the enormous wealth of our country for human needs? That is, should we begin to speak about ending war—not just this war or that war, but war itself?" He grasped that this is a matter of global survival: "The abolition of war has become not only desirable but absolutely necessary if the planet is to be saved."

Trained as a historian, Zinn had a unique ability to take the long view on social change. He would notice the fragility of governments and the possibility of breakthroughs when most of the rest of us would come down with a bad case of pessimism, or even resignation. That's one of the things that makes him so inspiring.

As he wrote in "A Chorus Against War": "There is a basic weakness in governments—however massive their armies, however wealthy their treasuries, however they control the information given to the public—because their power depends on the obedience of citizens, of soldiers, of civil servants, of journalists and writers and teachers and artists. When these people begin to suspect they have been deceived, and when they withdraw their support, the government loses its legitimacy, and its power."

Oh, how I wish Howard Zinn had been alive in the year 2011 to see this prophecy come true in the Arab Spring. And oh, how I wish he could have seen the worker uprising in Wisconsin and then the Occupy movement take hold in the United States—and around the world. As he told Barsamian, "You never know what spark is going to really result in a conflagration. . . . You have to do things, do things, do things; you have to light that match, light that match, light that match, not knowing how often it's going to sputter and go out and at what point it's going to take hold. That's what happened in the civil-rights movement, and that's what happens in other movements. Things take a long time. It requires patience, but not a passive patience—the patience of activism."

He would not have been surprised at all by the Occupy movement because he pinpointed, in "Operation Enduring War," what he called "the core problem: that there is immense wealth available, enough to care for the urgent needs of everyone on Earth, and that this wealth is being monopolized by a small number of individuals, who squander it on luxuries and war while millions die and more millions live in misery. This is a problem understood by people everywhere." They understand with "supreme clarity," he added, that "the world is run by the rich."

Zinn retained hope for a better system, and he wasn't afraid to call it socialism. "I want socialism to have a good name," he wrote in "A Murderous World." No defender of the Soviet Union, he upheld the vision of "Karl Marx, Eugene Debs, Emma Goldman, Helen Keller."

And like John Lennon, Howard Zinn wasn't afraid to call himself a dreamer. In "Changing Obama's Mindset," he wrote: "Yes, we're dreamers. We want it all. We want a peaceful world. We want an egalitarian world. We don't want war. We don't want capitalism. We want a decent society."

He had a soft spot for artists, actors, singers, filmmakers, and writers. "They wage the battle for justice in a sphere which is unreachable by the dullness of ordinary discourse," he wrote in "Artists of Resistance."

When Kurt Vonnegut died, I made the obvious call and urged Howard to write an appreciation. He delivered a lovely little eulogy. He wrote: "Kurt Vonnegut was often asked why he bothered writing. He answered this way: 'Many people need desperately to receive this message: I feel and think much as you do, care about many of the things you care about. . . . You are not alone.' Millions and millions of people, all over the world, reading him, do not feel alone. What could be a more important achievement?"

I feel less alone having known Howard Zinn through our editor-writer relationship. And I feel less alone having known Howard Zinn simply as a reader of his words.

You'll feel less alone too.

For me, this book has been an extra pleasure. It's been like spending another couple of evenings together with Howard. (I just wish I could go buy him another malt.)

Now it's your turn to enjoy his company.

1.

TO DISAGREE IS TO BE PUT ON THE ENEMIES LIST
June 1980

Think a bit about the history of these past twenty-five years in the United States—the years of the black revolt and the movements of women, prisoners, native Americans; the years of the great campaign against the Indochina war and the illumination of Watergate. It was in these twenty-five years that the Establishment began to lose control of the minds and the loyalties of the American people. And since about 1975, the Establishment has been working steadily, with some desperation, to reassert that control.

In those years of the movements, great numbers of Americans began to take democracy seriously—to think for themselves, to doubt the experts, to distrust the political leaders, and to lose faith in the military, the corporations and even the once-untouchable FBI and CIA. In mid-1975, the Harris poll, looking at the years since 1966, reported that public confidence in the military had dropped from 62 percent to 29 percent, in business from 55 percent to 18 percent, in the president and Congress from 42 percent to 13 percent. When the Survey Research Center of the University of Michigan posed the question, "Is the Government run by a few big interests looking out for themselves?" the answer in 1964 was "yes" from 53 percent of those polled.

Harvard political scientist Samuel Huntington reported to the Trilateral Commission—a group of Establishment intellectuals and political leaders from the United States, Europe, and Japan, assembled by David Rockefeller and Zbigniew Brezinski in the early 1970s—on what he called "The Democratic Distemper." "The 1960s witnessed a dramatic upsurge of democratic fervor in America," Huntington observed, and that troubled him. He noted that in 1960 only 18 percent of the public believed the government was spending too much on defense, but by 1969 this figure had jumped to 52 percent. He wrote: "The essence of the democratic surge of the 1960s was a general challenge to existing systems of authority, public and private. In one form or another, this challenge manifested itself in the family, the university, business, public and private associations, politics, the governmental bureaucracy, and the military services. People no longer felt the same obligation to obey those whom they had previously considered superior to themselves in age, rank, status, expertise, character, or talents."

Huntington was worried: "The question necessarily arises, however, whether if a new threat to security should materialize in the future (as it inevitably will at some point), the Government will possess the authority to command the resources, as well as the sacrifices, which are necessary to meet that threat." We were beset, he wrote, by "an excess of democracy." He suggested "desirable limits to the extension of political democracy."

Let us imagine the nation's elite addressing itself to

the problem posed by Huntington. If the proper respect for authority is to be regained, then surely the universities must do their job. It has usually been possible to count on them to fill the lower ranks of the Establishment with technical and professional people who, fairly well paid and engrossed in their own advancement, would serve as loyal guards for the system. But in the early 1960s, young black rebels came off the college campuses and formed the militant cutting edge of the black movement, and then the universities became the focal points of teach-ins and demonstrations against the war.

True, the loss of allegiance extended far beyond the campus, into the workplaces and homes of ordinary Americans, into the army ranks where working-class GIs turned against the war. Still, with twelve million young people in college, the fear of a working-class–profession-al-class coalition for social change makes it especially im-portant to educate for obedience. And the intensifying economic pressures of unemployment and inflation may suggest to the national elite that it is now easier, and also more necessary, to teach the teachers as well as the stu-dents the advisability of submitting to higher authority.

Thus, it may be part of some larger reordering of the nation's mind when the president of Boston University (BU), John Silber, says on national television (CBS's *60 Minutes*, viewed by thirty million), "A university should not be a democracy. . . . The more democratic a university is, the lousier it is."

As soon as Silber became BU's president in 1971, he began to act out his philosophy by destroying what is at the heart of humanistic education—the idea that students and faculty should have a decisive voice about the way education takes place. And he had an additional target—the idea that workers at the university should have some right to decide the conditions of their work.

Those of us who are involved in the intense, sometimes bizarre battles at Boston University have not had much time to step back and look for some grand national design into which we might fit. Furthermore, it seems immodest; we have not yet become accustomed to the fact that our campus, with its nondescript assortment of buildings straddling Commonwealth Avenue in the heart of the city, with its heterogeneous enrollment of 20,000 students, has begun to attract the attention of the country. It is as if a rare disease had broken out somewhere, and was being observed by everyone with much curiosity and a bit of apprehension.

John Silber, formerly a professor of philosophy at the University of Texas, had hardly settled into the presidential mansion—a twenty-room house, rent-free, only one of the many fringe benefits adding up to perhaps $100,000 a year which augment his $100,000 salary—when he embarked on the process the Germans call *Gleichschaltung*—"straightening things out." He quickly made it clear that he would not tolerate student interference with military recruiting at BU for the war in Vietnam. Early in 1972, his administration invited Marine Corps recruiters to a campus building. When students sat down on the steps of that building, remaining there firmly but peaceably, he called the police. Arrests and beatings followed, and Silber said he was maintaining "an open university."

The university that was "open" to the Marine Corps turned out to be closed to the campus chapter of Students for a Democratic Society (SDS), which lost its charter and its right to meet on campus because a scuffle had taken place during an SDS demonstration. The logic was established: SDS was a violent organization, while the Marine Corps had a well-known record for pacifism.

A series of demonstrations followed, to which police were called again and again, and which they broke up with arrests and brutal beatings. The turmoil led to a huge assembly of the Faculty Senate, which voted overwhelmingly that Marine Corps recruiting should be halted until faculty and students could discuss and vote on whether it should be resumed. Silber simply ignored the resolution. That summer, without the called-for campus discussion, he polled the faculty through the mail, not specifically asking about Marine Corps recruiting, but rather about whether the faculty wanted an "open university." The answer, of course, was yes, and the recruiters were on campus to stay.

That fall, the students did vote, in an unprecedented turnout. A large majority rejected the policy of military recruiting on campus. Silber ignored them too. Picketing students, he said, were "primates," and votes did not matter. "I would be much more impressed," he told the student newspaper, the *Daily Free Press*, "by a thoughtful document that was brought in by one single student than I would by a mindless referendum of 16,000." He would decide who was "thoughtful" and who was "mindless."

The centralization of power in Silber's hands, his contempt for faculty as well as students, his attempts to push tenured professors at the School of Theology into resigning, his repeated attacks on the tenure system—all this led to a burst of faculty unionization under the auspices of the American Association of University Professors

(AAUP). Silber, confident of his oratorical powers, went to faculty meetings at the various colleges, arguing that a vote for unionization would mean the end of the "collegial" model and the introduction of the "industrial" model at Boston University. Nonetheless, the faculty voted by a clear majority for a union. In the next four years, the Silber administration spent huge sums of money before the National Labor Relations Board (NLRB) and in the courts, trying unsuccessfully to overturn that vote.

Silber's argument against the AAUP was that well-paid and articulate college professors don't need a union. But when other employes tried to act in concert to improve their situation, his administration did its best to beat them down. Workers at the Student Health Clinic were fired when they met to voice grievances. The NLRB, after lengthy hearings, ruled that the BU administration was guilty of unfair labor practices in firing seven employes and intimidating the rest.

In the spring of 1976, departmental budget cuts led to anger on all sides.

Later, it was learned that while Silber was jacking up student tuition and telling the faculty there was no money for raises, he was putting several million dollars a year into "reserves" and listing these set-aside funds as "expenses" so that the budget barely showed a surplus.

There were calls for Silber's dismissal from ten of the fifteen deans, from faculties at various colleges in the university, from virtually every student organization, and finally from a Faculty Senate meeting. A committee of trustees, making its five-year evaluation of Silber, voted 7 to 1 that his contract should not be renewed. But he worked furiously at lining up trustee votes, found powerful allies on the board, and persuaded them to keep him in the presidency.

As part of the campaign for control, Silber began to put the screws to campus newspapers that criticized him. Advertising was withdrawn from the *BU News* (which had been a pioneering critic of the Vietnam War under the editorship of Ray Mungo), causing it to close. A new student publication called *Exposure*, pitilessly anti-Silber (one of its headlines referred to him as: "Mediocre Philosopher, Expert Chiseler"), had its funds—allocated from student activities fees—cut off. A new policy was adopted: Campus newspapers that wanted funding from student activities fees must submit to prior review of their copy by faculty advisers. Programs at the campus radio station, WBUR, came under scrutiny of Silber's administrators, and one news director was fired when he refused to censor the tape of a speech by William Kunstler which contained a joke about John Silber.

It also became more and more clear that any faculty member who spoke out against Silber was in danger of being denied tenure or, if tenured, of being denied a pay raise. Again and again, departmental recommendations of raises for certain faculty who were outspoken critics of the Silber administration were overruled. Early in Silber's administration, Professor Richard Newman, who had taught in the social sciences for nine years, resigned from the University, and told the *BU News* that budget cuts had eliminated almost half the faculty of his department, including "three or four of the best young teacher-scholars in the country." Newman said, "To disagree with the President is to be put on the Enemies List."

Students, faculty, and staff fought back. The *BU*

Exposure raised outside money to keep publishing its stories of administration shenanigans. There was evidence that Silber was pushing law school applicants to the top of the list when financial contributions from their families were sought. "I am not ashamed to sell these indulgences," he told a meeting of the trustees, and somehow the *Exposure* got hold of the transcript. It was a joke, Silber explained. And later, when the *Exposure* reprinted an administration memorandum in which a wealthy trustee was described as having sought and received "pre-admission" to the law school for his two small grandchildren "for the twenty-first century," Silber said that was a joke too—lots of jokes from an administration known for its utter lack of humor.

Clerical workers on campus, underpaid and harassed, began organizing a union and won an NLRB election. Librarians formed a union and won their election. The Silber administration refused to negotiate with them, as it had with the faculty union. When the buildings-and-grounds workers, long unionized, went on strike for a week in the fall of 1978, members of the other unions, along with students, formed large picket lines and held support rallies. They were getting ready for a big labor upsurge the following spring.

In April 1979, Boston University, whose employes were now probably the most organized of any private university in the country, became the most strike-ridden in the country. The administration, having exhausted its court appeals, had to enter into negotiations with the faculty union. It came to an agreement, under the faculty threat of an April strike deadline, then reneged on the agreement at the last moment.

The faculty called a strike that same evening. The next morning, the lines were up at twenty-one buildings. By noon, hundreds of picketing faculty were joined by clerical workers and librarians insisting that the administration negotiate with them on their own demands.

The Silber administration had not expected such a reaction. The strike quickly crippled the operations of the university. Of 800 faculty in the bargaining unit, at least 700 were observing the picket lines, and of these about 350 were picketing. It was a rare, perhaps unique event in the history of American higher education—professors and secretaries walking the picket lines together in a common strike.

After nine days, the administration and faculty agreed on a contract providing substantial wage increases and a grievance procedure, but leaving most decisions on tenure and other matters still in the hands of the president and trustees. The clerical workers and librarians were still on the picket lines.

With varying degrees of anguish, most of the faculty, feeling bound by a no-sympathy-strike clause in the contract, went back to work, but about seventy refused to cross the picket lines and held their classes out of doors or off campus. In nine more days, with the clerical workers and librarians holding firm, the administration agreed to negotiate, and everyone went back to work.

However, by late summer, the bargaining between the clerical workers and the administration broke down. Faculty and students returning for the fall semester found picket lines in place. It took a week for the strike to be settled by a contract agreement.

A small number of faculty had refused to cross the

clerical workers' picket lines and either held their classes elsewhere or had colleagues take their classes. Five of us— political scientist Murray Levin, journalist Caryl Rivers, historian Fritz Ringer (president of the faculty union during the spring strike), psychologist Andrew Dibner, and I— were warned that we had violated the no-sympathy-strike provision. We replied that we had acted as individuals, according to our consciences, in expressing our support for the clerical workers. The Silber administration announced it was proceeding against us under the contract—we were all tenured professors—utilizing a provision for the suspension or dismissal of tenured professors on grounds of "gross neglect of duty or other just cause."

The charges against the BU Five, as we came to be known, lent new urgency to the work of the Committee to Save BU, formed by faculty and students to rid the campus of the Silber machine.

Last December 18, a record number of faculty crowded into the largest auditorium on campus and listened to colleagues detail the charges against the Silber administration—mismanagement, centralization of decision-making, discrimination against women, violations of civil liberties and abusive and insulting behavior toward faculty.

Managers, whether of a government or of an institution, must learn how to gauge the capacity for rebellion so that they can head it off with the proper mix of repression and concession. The Silber administration had misjudged, when it reneged on the union contract in the spring of 1979, the faculty's willingness and readiness to strike. It misjudged again when it went after the BU Five. The threat to fire tenured faculty for honoring their convictions—Silber was quoted in the press as saying that faculty who signed union contracts had surrendered their right of conscience—aroused immediate protest.

Salvador Luria, Nobel laureate in biology at MIT and a veteran of the anti-war movement, began circulating a petition among faculty at MIT, Harvard, and other colleges and universities in the Boston area, calling for the charges against the Five to be dropped and for Silber to be fired. Five hundred faculty in the Boston area signed the petition within two weeks. Another petition, signed by Luria, Noam Chomsky, historian John Womack of Harvard and historian of science Everett Mendelsohn of Harvard, began circulating nationwide. The signatures came pouring in.

Alumni wrote letters to the BU trustees and the Boston newspapers. On campus, student groups called for the charges to be dropped and for Silber's removal.

The Massachusetts Community College Council, representing faculty at fifteen colleges, protested. A sociologist withdrew his request to be a visiting professor at BU, citing the administration's action. The Massachusetts Sociological Association passed a resolution expressing its concern for "freedom of conscience." A visiting linguistics professor from Paris brought word back to France and a telegram came shortly after, signed by fifteen distinguished French academicians, declaring their support for the BU Five.

But the slick pro-Silber profile on *60 Minutes* drew letters of support from viewers around the country who saw Silber as the man who would make the dirty college kids clean up their rooms and whip the radical faculty into line.

This spring, Silber still seems to have a firm grasp on his Commonwealth Avenue fiefdom. The trustees have given no overt signs of disaffection. The faculty union is entangled in a hundred grievances in the slow machinery of the contract. BU students, just handed an outrageous 16 percent tuition increase, are only beginning to organize. The threat of punishment still keeps many faculty in line. Indeed, the dean of the College of Liberal Arts has announced he is adding a new factor in determining merit raises: A faculty member's teaching performance and publications, however stellar, may be offset, he says, by "negative merit"—actions designed to "harm the University."

There are some signs, however, that the protests from all over the academic world are having an effect. In February, the administration, through the intercession of a committee appointed by the official Faculty Council, agreed to drop the charges against the BU Five, and to negotiate or arbitrate the question of punishment for faculty refusal to cross picket lines.

After six members of the Committee to Save BU appeared before the trustees—in an unprecedented contact with a board always remote from the faculty—it was learned that there were expressions of disaffection among the trustees, who have been Silber's last stronghold.

The board has welcomed Silber's enthusiasm for the banking and utilities interests they represent, as well as his friendliness toward the military. Silber has been a spokesman for nuclear power and against the evening out of utility rates to favor the small consumer. Boston University has an overseas program in which it services the American military with courses and degrees, and

Silber has shown obvious deference to the government's military needs in ROTC and recruiting.

Nevertheless, as faculty, secretaries, librarians and buildings-and-grounds workers remain organized and determined to fight back, as students become increasingly resentful at being treated like peons in a banana republic, as protests from alumni and from the national academic community intensify, the trustees may have to reconsider. When risks become too great, the clubs of the Establishment sometimes decide to change to a form of control less crass and more conciliatory. To prevent more drastic upheaval, the board may replace Silber with its own version of a Gerald Ford or Jimmy Carter.

Back in 1976, John Silber wrote on the op-ed page of the *New York Times*: "As Jefferson recognized, there is a natural aristocracy among men. The grounds of this are virtue and talent. . . . Democracy freed from a counterfeit and ultimately destructive egalitarianism provides a society in which the wisest, the best, and the most dedicated assume positions of leadership. . . . As long as intelligence is better than stupidity, knowledge than ignorance, and virtue than vice, no university can be run except on an elitist basis."

That makes for a neat fit with the philosophy of Samuel Huntington and the Trilateral Commission as they react to the "excess of democracy" that sprang from the movements of the 1960s. The Establishment's need to reassert control over the universities expresses itself most blatantly in the authoritarianism of John Silber at Boston University, but there is some evidence of a national trend in higher education toward the punishment of dissent and toward more direct intervention by big business in the workings of the universities. Earlier this year, the *New York Times* reported that schools of business around the country—at Dartmouth, Duke, and Cornell, among others—now have "executives-in-residence" to match the more customary university practice of maintaining "artists-in-residence" and "writers-in-residence." And the American Council on Education has been urging colleges to recruit more aggressively and to increase their ties to business. Management and marketing consultants are now a common presence on campuses, as are union-busting consultants and "security" advisers.

As the economic situation of the universities becomes more precarious and faculties shrink, it becomes easier to get rid of undesirables, whether political dissidents or just troublesome campus critics. If they are untenured, dismissal is a simple process. If they are tenured, some ingenuity is required. The files of the American Association of University Professors show, according to one member of the AAUP's committee on academic freedom, "a disturbing number of mean little cases this year." He said, "There seem to be many tenth-rate John Silbers around."

The AAUP refers to an increasing number of "indecencies." At Central Washington State University, a tenured professor of political science, Charles Stasny, was recently fired by the trustees for "insubordination" after he missed several classes because he attended a scholarly meeting in Israel. The administration had first approved his departure, then opposed it. At Nichols College, outside Worcester, Massachusetts, a non-tenured professor who questioned the leadership of the college president was summarily dismissed. At Philander Smith College in Little Rock, two tenured professors and one non-tenured faculty member were fired last June and told to leave the campus the same day; they had complained to student newspapers and the trustees about the lack of academic freedom on campus.

Whether at universities or at other workplaces, whether in the United States or in other countries, we seem to face the same challenge: The corporations and the military, shaken and frightened by the rebellious movements of recent decades, are trying to reassert their undisputed power. We have a responsibility not only to resist, but to build on the heritage of those movements, and to move toward the ideals of egalitarianism, community, and self-determination—whether at work, in the family, or in the schools—which have been the historic, unfulfilled promise of the word *democracy*.

2.

A MURDEROUS WORD
February 1989

In 1948, the House Committee on Un-American Activities distributed a pamphlet entitled *One Hundred Things You Should Know About Communism*.

(I found a copy in my files. They kept files on me; I kept files on them. It's only fair.)

The pamphlet had 100 questions and answers.

"Question 1: What is Communism?"

"Answer: A system by which one small group seeks to rule the world."

The answer was probably drawn up by the people who later founded the Trilateral Commission.

Let me skip to Question 76. "Where can a Communist be found in everyday life?" (This question particularly interested me, because there have been times when I was in need of a communist.)

"Answer: Look for him in your school, your labor union, your church, or your civic club."

"Question 86: Is the YMCA a Communist target?" (This really worries me. I have always wondered why there was so much chlorine in the YMCA swimming pool.)

"Answer: Yes, so is the YWCA."

The history of anticommunism is such a rich, poor history. I'm thinking of Representative Harold Velde of Illinois, who stood up in the House to oppose money for mobile libraries in rural areas. He said, "Educating Americans through the means of the library service could bring about a change in their political attitude quicker than any other method. The basis of communism and socialistic influence is education of the people."

Or take Joseph Papp, who was being questioned by the House Un-American Activities Committee. Asked whether he had ever introduced any communist stuff into his plays, he replied, "Well, I do Shakespeare." Richard Arens, the staff director, interposed: "We are not saying that William Shakespeare was a communist."

Let's skip to 1987 and the Iran-contra investigation. Robert McFarlane, the national-security adviser to the president, said he knew the policy of getting arms to the contras illegally wouldn't work—not that it was wrong, but it wouldn't work. He said, "Succinctly put, where I went wrong was in not having the guts to stand up and tell the President that. To tell you the truth, probably the reason I didn't is because if I had done that, Bill Casey, Jeane Kirkpatrick, and Cap Weinberger would have said I was some kind of commie, you know."

Robert McFarlane, some kind of a commie?

While it is a little bizarre, a little laughable, anticommunism represents something terribly serious. *Communism* is one of those words that are calculated to stop rational discourse, words that are murderous.

The word is used to prop up dictatorships all over the world, to invade other countries, to bomb peasant villages, to destroy an economy of a small neighboring country (I'm talking about Nicaragua), and to rob the hard-earned salaries of so many Americans to finance these trillions of dollars worth of stupid weapons.

During the Vietnam War, the term *communist* was used to justify everything: a ten-year war, the dropping of seven million bombs, the dispatch of 500,000 troops, and the destruction of a country.

A man named Charles Hutto told U.S. Army criminal investigators, "I remember the unit's combat assault on My Lai 4. The night before the mission we had a briefing by Captain Medina. He said, "Everything in the village was communist.' So we shot men, women, and children."

Murderous words. The use of the word *communism* was designed to stop rational discussion, even rational discussion of communism. I think we do need a sober, serious discussion of communism and socialism. We need a discussion of the Soviet Union, we need criticism of the Soviet Union. I believe we need anger and indignation at the Soviet Union for some of the things that have been done to people over there.

The policies of the Soviet Union have given socialism a bad name, and I want socialism to have a good name. Socialism to me got a good name from Karl Marx, Eugene Debs, Emma Goldman, Helen Keller (a lot of people don't know Helen Keller was a socialist, how she was redbaited, how she was put down because of her views).

But there's a difference between the kind of reasonable criticism you could have of communism and socialism as practiced in the Soviet Union and other states and the kind of murderous, indiscriminate hatred that leads us to threaten to drop bombs and kill all of the citizens of these countries. We're apparently prepared to kill all of them to save them, as we have always been prepared to kill people to save them from communism.

This country does not react the same way now to the word *communism* as it did when the Vietnam War had just begun.

Listen to the later thoughts of Hutto, the infantryman who was at My Lai and who now has a wife and two children: "I was nineteen years old and I was always told to do what the Government, what grownups had told me to do. But now I'll tell my son, if the Government calls, use your own judgment. Now I don't think there should even be a thing called war, because it messes up a person's mind."

As a result of the Vietnam War, millions of Americans have learned to think twice about the cry of communism; that's why the American people are not ready to support an invasion of Nicaragua just because it is "a Marxist dictatorship and communism is bad and it's on our southern flank" (which is, you know, a very deft threat to our biological functions). People don't really go along with that. They can't whip up sentiments the way they used to.

There is so much to do, so many problems to solve. We need an open debate—no holds barred—of communism, socialism, capitalism, democracy, liberty, everything.

Nobody should be afraid. People accused of liberalism should not be afraid.

People accused of communism should not be afraid.

We should talk about class, we should talk about internationalism, we should talk about racism, we should talk about one world, we should talk about unilateral disarmament.

Nothing should stand in the way.

3.

ORGANIZING THE ORGANIZED
November 1990

The progressive movement in the United States has been unnecessarily thrown for a loop by the recent events in Eastern Europe. That is, we are accepting the Establishment's caricature of us—that our hopes for democratic socialism, or for participatory democracy, or for an egalitarian society (any of these descriptions will do) rested in some way on the bureaucratic pseudo-Marxist societies in the Soviet Union and Eastern Europe. That may have been true of the communist movement of the 1930s and 1940s, and may still be true of some far-left groups today, but it does not apply to the broad civil-rights, anti-war, feminist, environmental, gay-rights movement that swept the country in the 1960s and continues today in various forms. Those movements were a *new* Left—isn't that what we called ourselves?—which was critical of the Soviet Union and of dictatorship everywhere.

Those movements were based on certain fundamental ideas: racial equality, antimilitarism, sexual equality, economic democracy, a suspicion of all state power, and a true cultural revolution in the schools, in family life, in human relations.

So we need to shake off the burden laid on us, which

we have foolishly accepted, of bearing responsibility for the distortions of socialism in various parts of the world. And we need to set out boldly to declare our own agenda. This means making clear (if it has not been clear heretofore) that we never were and are not supporters of a bureaucratic, dictatorial pseudo-socialism. But this does not mean, as the Establishment is rushing to declare, that the alternative is a happy return to laissez-faire capitalism.

We have before us the job of deflating those romantic ideas of the beauties of capitalism which are being rushed off the production line and shipped to those countries that have recently gone through tumultuous change and are looking for new ideas. We need to remind everyone (and ourselves) that capitalism is an *old* idea, and one which caused so much misery that it led people all over the world to turn in desperation to solutions that themselves turned out to be disastrous.

We have an educational job to do. We must point out that the only reason capitalism was able to survive in the Western world is that its victims *organized*—in trade-union movements, in farmers' movements, in tenants' movements, in women's movements, in civil-rights movements—and brought about just enough reforms (the eight-hour day, old-age pensions, higher pay, unemployment insurance, civil-rights laws, women's suffrage) to stave off revolution and leave capitalism alive, with a surface of great prosperity and a core of economic and cultural sickness. And we must point out that in the era of capitalism, whatever "progress" was made for new middle classes, starvation remained for most of the world, and national rivalries brought the most murderous wars in history.

So our job today is to *organize*, to create a vast movement in our country that can link up with popular movements in other countries of the world. The irresistible popular movements for change in Czechoslovakia, Poland, East Germany, and elsewhere in Eastern Europe, the great populist surges that toppled the Shah in Iran, Ferdinand Marcos in the Philippines, dictatorships in Latin America; the black movement in South Africa, the Palestinian upsurge in the Occupied Territories—all this is evidence of the *potential* for democratic revolutions everywhere. And it should not be impossible, though it will not be easy, to persuade Americans that our society, too, despite its glitter of consumer goods, needs the kind of democratic revolution we have been exulting over as we have watched events in Europe.

It should not be impossible to persuade Americans that such a democratic revolution is needed, when wealth is more and more concentrated at the top, when the economy is unhealthy, when we are ridden by homelessness, by frightening violence in our cities, by pervasive drug addiction, by alcoholism, by a deteriorating, poisonous environment—in short, when we show all the signs of a rich but sick society.

By *organize* I mean, to a great extent, organizing the organized. There already exist thousands upon thousands of organizations all over this country, representing millions of people—Greenpeace alone has two million members—working for peace, racial equality, consumer protection, environmental health, women's rights, and other important causes. What can link them together (loosely, fitfully, without disturbing their identity, but joining their powers for certain crucial campaigns, as when so many different groups joined to block the nomination of Robert Bork to the Supreme Court) is a simple common agenda.

That agenda is: using the immense wealth that goes each year into the military ($200 billion of the $300 billion, as an arbitrary starting point) and showing in detail how this $200 billion can give us: universal health care, guaranteed housing for everyone, useful work for everyone capable of working, child care for all working mothers, a cleanup of air and water all over the country, subsidies for the arts, a doubling of teachers' salaries, and more.

The American public has already shown, in various public opinion surveys, that it will support reductions in military expenditures. The fading of the "Soviet threat" now makes possible a radical proposal for de-militarization to rebuild American society.

The foreign-policy agenda is a bold, simple one: renunciation of force in the solution of international problems; the substitution of nonmilitary solutions, whether economic pressure or negotiation, on the grounds that recent history shows no gains for human rights through military solutions, whether in Vietnam, Afghanistan, Nicaragua, El Salvador, or the Middle East.

4.

OUTSIDE THE CLASSROOM:
INTERVIEW WITH DAVID BARSAMIAN
July 1997

Howard Zinn is a model of the activist scholar. He grew up class-conscious in a poor immigrant family. "We were always," he recalls, "one step ahead of the landlord." There were no books or magazines at home. The first book he remembers reading was *Tarzan and the Jewels of Opar*. He found it in the street, the first ten pages ripped out. But it didn't matter to him. When his parents discovered his interest in books, they took advantage of a newspaper offer and ordered the complete works of Charles Dickens. Later they got him a used Underwood No. 5 typewriter. The rest is history.

Even though he earned Ph.D. from Columbia, Zinn learned of the Ludlow Massacre in Colorado only by hearing a Woody Guthrie song about the event. That omission in his education taught him a lot about what is included and excluded in conventional textbooks.

Zinn is an excavator and memory retriever. He recovers valuable and hidden aspects of the past. The lessons inform us, and they inspire us to social action.

He also has a keen interest in the arts. His play *Emma*,

on the life of Emma Goldman, has been performed in New York, Boston, London, Edinburgh, and Tokyo. His most recent play is *Marx in Soho*.

At seventy-five, Zinn is as active as ever. The professor emeritus at Boston University is in great demand as a speaker all over the country. But in characteristic fashion, he doesn't just speak. He acts as well. He recently was arrested in Everett, Massachusetts, in support of Salvadoran women workers at a curtain factory.

Zinn is one of the most beloved figures in the progressive movement. And he's proof that you can be radical and have a sense of humor. I talked with him in the offices of the Harvard Trade Union Program in Cambridge.

Q: In your memoir, you write of an incident in Times Square that had a big political impact on you.
Howard Zinn: I was a seventeen-year-old kid living in the slums of Brooklyn. Living on the same block were these young communists who were older than I and seemed very politically sophisticated. They asked me to come to a demonstration at Times Square. I had never been to a demonstration, and going to Times Square sounded very exciting. I went along.

It seemed like nothing was going on. But my friend said, "Wait." The clock on the *New York Times* building said ten.

Suddenly, banners unfurled all around me. People started marching down the street. It was very exciting. I wasn't even sure what it was all about, except that vaguely I thought that it was against war.

At some point there were two women in front of us carrying banners. This was before the age of feminist consciousness, even among leftists. My friends said, "We mustn't let these two women carry this banner. You take one end. I'll take the other end." It was like Charlie Chaplin picking up that red flag, a railroad signal flag, and suddenly there's this army of unemployed people marching behind him in this demonstration.

Then I heard these sirens. I thought there must be a fire somewhere around. But no. The mounted police arrived, driving their horses into the crowd, beating the people. It was a wild scene. Before I knew it, I was spun around by the shoulder, hit, and knocked unconscious.

I woke up, I don't know how much later, in a doorway. Times Square was back as it was before. It was very eerie, as if nothing had happened. My friend was gone. The demonstration was over. The police were gone.

I was nursing not only a hurt head, but hurt feelings about our country. All the things these radicals had been saying were true. The state is not neutral, but on the side of the powerful; there really is no freedom of speech in this country if you're a radical. That was brought home to me, because these people were engaging in a nonviolent demonstration, presumably protected by the Constitution and—zoom!—the police are there beating heads and breaking up the demonstration.

Q: The title of your memoir is You Can't Be Neutral on a Moving Train. *Why did you pick a title like that?*
Zinn: To confuse people, so that everybody who introduces me at a lecture gets it all wrong, like *You Can't Be Training in a Neutral Place*. The title came out of my classroom teaching, where I would start off my classes explaining to my students—because I didn't want to deceive

them—that I would be taking stands on everything. They would hear my point of view in this course, that this would not be a neutral course. My point to them was that in fact it was impossible to be neutral. *You Can't Be Neutral on a Moving Train* means that the world is already moving in certain directions. Things are already happening. Wars are taking place. Children are going hungry. In a world like this—already moving in certain, often terrible directions—to be neutral or to stand by is to collaborate with what is happening. I didn't want to be a collaborator, and I didn't want to invite my students to be collaborators.

Q: Was your job at Spelman College in Atlanta a radicalizing experience for you? I presume you lived in a black neighborhood near the college.

Zinn: Actually, the first year we were there, 1956, we lived in a white, working-class neighborhood on the edge of Atlanta, which was an interesting experience in itself. We weren't far from Stone Mountain, which is a Ku Klux Klan gathering place.

One of the first things that happened when we were there is we heard all this noise. We went outside. There was a main street about a block from our house. There was a parade of people with white hoods, KKK, marching to Stone Mountain.

We moved to the Spelman College campus, which was surrounded by a black community. We lived in the black community for the next six years. Probably that time at Spelman College was the most intense experience of learning in my life. Talk about social change: I could see social change happening all around me. I was writing about it, observing it, participating in it. My Spelman

College students—especially young black women—were being trained to take their obedient places in the segregated society. Trained to pour tea and wear white gloves and march into and out of chapel.

Then suddenly I saw them break away from this after they watched the sit-ins taking place in Greensboro and Rock Hill and Nashville, and I saw them getting together and planning the first sit-ins in the spring of 1960 in Atlanta.

This was remarkable—this growth of courage and getting arrested, going to jail. I saw my students literally leaping over that stone wall that surrounded Spelman College campus and doing what they weren't supposed to do.

I saw Marian Wright Edelman, my student at Spelman, go to jail. A photo of her appeared in the newspapers the next day showing this very studious Spelman student behind bars reading a book which she brought along with her so she wouldn't miss her homework.

I participated in sit-ins, and I saw the atmosphere around us in Rich's department store suddenly change from friendly to hostile when four of us—two black and two white, my wife and I and two black students from Spelman—sat down at this lunch counter. Suddenly it was as if a bomb had been dropped or a plague had been visited on it. The people gathering around us were shouting and cursing. I got an inkling of what it is to be black and be subject all your life to the thought that if you step one foot out of line you'll be surrounded by people who are threatening you.

I saw the South change in that time. White Southerners getting used to the idea that the South was going to change and accepting it.

I learned a lot about teaching, too. I learned that the most important thing about teaching is not what you do in the classroom but what you do outside of the classroom. You go outside the classroom yourself, bring your students outside, or have them bring you outside the classroom, because very often they do it first and you say, "I can't hang back. I'm their teacher. I have to be there with them." And you learn that the best kind of teaching makes this connection between social action and book learning.

Q: Do you miss teaching?
Zinn: I miss the classroom and the encounter with students. But I'm not completely divorced from that situation, because now that I'm not teaching in a formal way, I do go around the country and speak to groups of young people, and do a kind of teaching. I love to speak to high school students. As a result, I don't miss teaching as much as I might have if I simply retired from teaching and played tennis.

Q: Why do you think so many of your colleagues want to just busy themselves with their scholarship and churn out papers and attend conferences? I'm not saying that doesn't have any value. But when it comes to being "out there," to being engaged with what's happening in the streets, in society, they don't feel it's appropriate.
Zinn: In our society, there's a powerful drive for safety and security. Everybody is vulnerable because we are all part of a hierarchy of power. Unless we're at the very, very top, unless we're billionaires, unless we're the president of the United States, unless we're the boss, and very

few of us are bosses, we are somewhere on some lower rung in the hierarchy of power. If somebody has power over us, somebody has the power to fire us, to withhold a raise, to punish us in some way.

Here in this rich country, so prideful of the economic system, the most clear-cut thing you can say is that everybody is insecure. Everybody is nervous. Even if you're doing well, you're nervous. Something will happen to you. In fact, the people who are doing fairly well, the middle class, are more nervous than the people at the bottom, who know what to expect. The academic world has its own special culture of conformity and being professional. Being professional means not being committed.

It's unprofessional to be a teacher who goes out on picket lines, or who invites students out on picket lines, unprofessional to be a teacher who says to students, "Look, instead of giving you a final exam of multiple-choice questions asking you who was president during the Mexican War, your assignment is to go out into the community and work with some organization that you believe in and then do a report on that."

And you will stand out. You will stick out if the stuff you write is not written for scholarly journals but is written for everybody. Certainly the stuff written for scholarly journals is deliberately written in such a way that very few people can read it. So if you write stuff that an ordinary person can read, you're suspect. They'll say you're not a scholar, you're a journalist. Or you're not a scholar, you're a propagandist, because you have a point of view. Of course, scholarly articles have a point of view. They have an agenda. But they may not even know they have an agenda. The agenda is obedience. The agenda is silence. The agenda is safety. The agenda is "Don't rock the boat."

Q: *Have you noticed any changes in your profession, history?*
Zinn: No question there have been changes. Not changes enough to say that the teaching of history has changed. But obviously enough changes to alarm the right wing in this country, to alarm the American Legion, to alarm senators, to alarm Lynne Cheney, Robert Dole, William Bennett, Gertrude Himmelfarb, and to alarm all these people who are holding on to the old history.

The story of Columbus has changed now, not in the majority of schools around the country, but in thousands. This is alarming. What? Young kids are going to begin to think of Columbus as not just an adventurer, but as a predator, a kidnapper, an enslaver, a torturer, a bad person, and think maybe that conquest and expansion are not good things and that the search for gold is not something to be welcomed? Kids, be happy! Gold has been found!

And maybe, let's take a look at the Indian societies Columbus came upon. How did they live? How did they treat one another? Columbus stories told in the schools don't usually tell about how the Indians were living on this continent.

Somebody sent me a letter reminding me of the work of William Brandon. He has done research for decades about Indians and their communities in this hemisphere before Columbus came and after. It's an amazing story, and one that would make anybody question capitalism, greed, competition, disparate wealth, hierarchy. To start to hint about that, telling a new kind of Columbus story, a new kind of Native American story, is subversive.

Also, the Reconstruction period is being told in a new way. Eric Foner's book *Reconstruction* is marvelous. It's a very different treatment of Reconstruction than when I was going to graduate school in the 1950s, where incidentally they did not put on my reading list W. E. B. DuBois's *Black Reconstruction*, which is a vital predecessor to Eric Foner's book.

So a lot of history teaching has changed. Not enough. But just enough to frighten the keepers of the old.

Q: Some years ago, speaking to a gathering of university presidents, John Silber, the chancellor of Boston University, talked darkly about those teachers who "poison the well of academe." His two chief examples? Noam Chomsky and Howard Zinn.

Zinn: I guess Silber thinks that there is some kind of pure well, then along come people like Chomsky and me and ruin it. That is the kind of accusation now being made in a larger sense about education by the right wing in this country, who claim that education was wonderful before the multiculturalists came in, before we had feminist studies and black studies and Native American studies and Chicano studies. The well was pure before students had to read *The Autobiography of Malcolm X* alongside Thomas Hardy, before they were given *I, Rigoberta Menchú* alongside Tolstoy and Rousseau.

But it was not a very pure well. It was pure only in the sense of the racial purity that was so talked about during the fascist years—a well that I would argue was itself poisonous. It perpetuated an education that left out large numbers of the world's people.

Q: Here's an easy one: How does social change happen?
Zinn: Thanks, David. I can deal with that in thirty seconds. You think I know? What I try to do is look at historical situations and extrapolate. You see change happening when there has been an accumulation of grievance until it reaches a boiling point. Then something happens. What happened in the South in the 1950s and 1960s? It's not that suddenly black people were put back into slavery. It's not as if there was some precipitating thing that suddenly pushed them back. They were, as the Southern white ruling class was eager to say, making progress. It was glacial progress, extremely slow. But they were making progress. But the ideal in the minds of the black people was "We have to be equal. We have to be treated as equals." The progress that was being made in the South was far from that. The recognition of that gap—between what should be and what is—existed for a long time but waited for a moment when a spark would be lit.

You never know what spark is going to really result in a conflagration. After all, before the Montgomery Bus Boycott there had been other boycotts. Before the sit-ins of the 1960s, there had been sit-ins in sixteen different cities between 1955 and 1960 that nobody paid any attention to and that did not ignite a movement.

But then in Greensboro, on February 1, 1960, these four college kids sit in, and everything goes haywire. Then things are never the same.

I think this is an encouragement to people who do things not knowing whether they will result in anything. You do things again and again, and nothing happens. You have to do things, do things, do things; you have to light that match, light that match, light that match, not knowing how often it's going to sputter and go out and at what point it's going to take hold. That's what happened in the civil-rights movement, and that's what happens in other movements. Things take a long time. It requires patience, but not a passive patience—the patience of activism.

When I was in South Africa in 1982, it was very, very interesting. We know about books being banned; there, people were banned. They couldn't speak. They couldn't go here or there. The secret police were everywhere. Just before I arrived at the University of Capetown, the secret police of South Africa had broken into the offices of the student newspaper at the University of Capetown and made off with all of their stuff. It was the kind of thing that happened all the time. There was an atmosphere of terror. You would think, perhaps, that nothing is going to happen here. But having come from that experience in the South, I was aware that underneath the surface of total control things were simmering; things were going on. I didn't know when it would break through, but we saw it break through not long ago. Suddenly Mandela comes out of Robben Island and becomes president of the new South Africa.

We should be encouraged by historical examples of social change, by how surprising changes take place suddenly, when you least expect it, not because of a miracle from on high, but because people have labored patiently for a long time.

When people get discouraged because they do something and nothing happens, they should really understand that the only way things will happen is if people get over the notion that they must see immediate success. If they get over that notion and persist, then they will see things happen before they even realize it.

Q: Let's talk about the American left and its values. What are left values to you?
Zinn: When I think of left values I think of socialism—not in the Soviet sense, not in the bureaucratic sense, not in the Bolshevik sense, but socialism in the sense of Eugene Debs and Mother Jones and Emma Goldman and anarchist socialists. Left values are fundamentally egalitarian values. If I had to say what is at the center of left values, it's the idea that everyone has a fundamental right to the good things in life, to the necessary things of life, that there should be no disproportions in the world.

It doesn't mean perfect equality; we can't possibly achieve that. I notice that your sweater is better than mine. But we both have a sweater, which is something.

The Declaration of Independence—the idea that everybody has an equal right to life, liberty, and the pursuit of happiness—to me is a remarkable statement of left values. Of course, in the Declaration of Independence it was all men. It had to be extended as the feminists of 1848 did when they created a new Declaration that added "women" to it. Now it has to be extended internationally.

One of the crucial values that the left must embrace is a value of international solidarity and equality across national lines. That's very important, because it changes everything if you begin to understand that the lives of children in other countries are equivalent to the lives of children in our country. Then war is impossible.

Just speaking around the country, presenting what I think are left values, I talk about the equal right of everybody to these things and about extending the principles of the Declaration of Independence all over the world. I find that people everywhere I go—and these are not captive audiences of just left-wing people; these are assemblies of people, a thousand high-school students who are assembled forcibly to hear me—they agree with this. It makes sense. It seems right. It seems moral.

They find themselves then accepting what they didn't accept before, for instance, the fact that you might say the dropping of the bomb on Hiroshima can be a controversial issue within the limits of discussion that have generally been set in our society. But if you change those limits by simply introducing the idea that the children of Japan have an equal right to life with the children of the United States, then suddenly it is impossible to drop a bomb in Hiroshima, just as it would be impossible to drop a bomb on the children of New York, even in order to end World War II faster.

Q: Talk about the idea of equality of opportunity, which is a big theme, versus equality of condition and then the outcome.
Zinn: The conservatives, and sometimes the liberals, make a big thing of, "Oh, well, what we just want to give people is equality of opportunity. We'll give them an education, and we'll send them out into the world and see what happens." Basically that's it. "We've done our best. And now let the fittest survive." It's a Darwinian idea. Our values should be that people should have health care and housing and work and food and an education, the fundamental things they need, and that should be guaranteed. To say we're giving people opportunity consigns to poverty those people who don't have, let's say, money-

making skills, moneymaking intelligence: the special kind of qualities that enable some people to become millionaires. These people may be poets or musicians, or they may just be decent people, or they may be carpenters, and so on. But they won't have a chance. So it's very important to rid ourselves of the notion that it's sufficient to give people so-called equality of opportunity.

Q: You've said, "We can't go on with the present polarization of wealth and poverty." Why not?
Zinn: I don't know how long we can go on, but I know we can't go on indefinitely. That growing gap between wealth and poverty is a recipe for trouble, for disaster, for conflict, for explosion. Here's the Dow Jones average going up, up, up, and there are the lives of people in the city. The Dow Jones average in the last fifteen years has gone up 400 percent. In the same period, the wages of the working population have gone down 15 percent. Now the richest 1 percent of the population owns 43–44 percent of the wealth. Up from the usual maybe 28 percent, 30 percent, 32 percent, which is bad enough and which has been a constant throughout American history. When they did studies of the tax rolls in Boston in the seventeenth century, they concluded that 1 percent of the population owned 33 percent of the wealth. If you look at the statistics all through American history, you see that figure, a little more, a little less, around the same. Now it's worse and worse. Something's got to give.

Q: So despite what the pundits are telling us about the population being passive and quiescent, you think there's an audience there for dissidence?

Zinn: Absolutely. Five hundred people come to hear me in Duluth, Minnesota. They're not people who are already aficionados of the left and of radical messages. They come maybe out of curiosity. Their interest has been piqued by an article in the newspaper or whatever, and they come to hear me.

Then I deliver what I believe is a radical message: This is what's wrong with our economic system. This is what's wrong with our political system. It's fundamental. We need to redistribute the wealth in this country. We need to use it in a rational way. We need to take this enormous arms budget and not just cut it slightly but dismantle it because we have to make up our minds we're not going to war anymore. We're not going to intervene militarily anymore. If we're not going to go to war any more, then we have $250 billion. We don't have to worry about Medicare, Social Security, child care, universal health care, education. We can have a better society.

I say things which, if you mentioned them on *The NewsHour with Jim Lehrer*, they would say, "That's a little too much for our listeners." It's not too much. You tell people what makes common sense. It makes common sense that if you're a very, very rich country that nobody should be hungry. Nobody should be homeless. Nobody should be without health care. The richest country in the world. Nobody should be without these things. We have the resources but they're being wasted or given somewhere to somebody. It's common sense. So there are people all over this country, millions of people, who would listen to such a message and say, "Yes, yes, yes."

5.
ONE IRAQI'S STORY
February 1999

As Bill Clinton and Tony Blair were bombing Iraq on December 20, I received an e-mail message from England:

Dear Professor Zinn,
I am an Iraqi citizen who sought refuge here in the U.K. because of the brutality of Saddam's regime, which, within two years, killed my innocent old father and my youngest brother, who left a wife and three children. . . .

I am writing to you to let you know that during the second day of bombarding Iraq, a cruise missile hit my parents' house in a suburb of Baghdad. My mother, my sister-in-law (wife of my deceased brother), and her three children were all killed instantly.

Such a tragedy shocked me to such an extent I lost my tears. I am crying without tears. I wish I could show my eyes and express my severe and painful suffering to every American and British [citizen]. I wish I could tell my story to those sitting in the American Administration, the U.N., and at Number 10 Downing Street. For the sake of Monica and Clinton, my family has to pay this expensive and invaluable cost. I am wondering, who will compensate me for my loss? I wish I could go to Iraq to drop some tears on my mother's grave, who always wanted to see me before her death. . . .

Please convey my story to all those whom you think can still see the truth in their eyes and can hear this tragic story with their ears.

Sincerely yours,

Dr. Mohammed Al-Obaidi

It seems to me this conveys with terrible clarity that Saddam Hussein and the leaders of our government have much in common: They are both visiting death and suffering on the people of Iraq.

In response to the possibility that Saddam Hussein may have "weapons of mass destruction" and the additional possibility that he may use them in the future, the United States, in the present, shows no compunction about using weapons of mass destruction: cruise missiles, B-52 bombers, and, most of all, economic sanctions, which have resulted in the deaths of hundreds of thousands of Iraqi children.

In the December bombings, Bill Clinton was perfectly willing to kill a number (how many we do not know) of Iraqis, including five members of Dr. Mohammed Al-Obaidi's family. Why? "To send a message," his administration said.

Would the United States be willing to take the lives of a similar number of Americans "to send a message"? Are Iraqis less worthy of life than we are? Are their children less innocent than ours?

President Clinton said that Saddam Hussein poses a "clear and present danger" to the peace of the world. Whatever danger Saddam Hussein may pose in the future, he is not a clear and present danger to the peace of the world. We are. Notice the president's use of this much-abused term. The Supreme Court of the United States invoked it to justify the imprisonment of people distributing leaflets protesting the U.S. entrance into World War I. Cold Warriors used it to justify McCarthyism and the nuclear arms race. Now President Clinton has pulled it off the shelf for equally disreputable purposes.

President Clinton also said that other nations besides Iraq have weapons of mass destruction, but Iraq alone has used them. He could say this only to a population deprived of history. No nation in the world possesses greater weapons of mass destruction than we do, and none has used them more often, or with greater loss of civilian life. In Hiroshima and Nagasaki, more than 100,000 civilians died after the United States dropped atom bombs on them. In Korea and Vietnam, millions died after the United States dropped "conventional" weapons on them. So who are we to brag about our restraint in using weapons of mass destruction?

The U.S. penchant for bombing blots out the government's ability to focus on humanitarian crises—and not just in Iraq. When Hurricane Mitch devastated Central America, leaving tens of thousands dead and more than a million people homeless, there was a desperate need for helicopters to transport people to safety and deliver food and medicine. Mexico supplied sixteen helicopters to Honduras. The United States supplied twelve. At the same time, the Pentagon dispatched a huge armada—helicopters, transport planes, B-52s—to the Middle East.

Every cruise missile used to bomb Iraq cost about $1 million, and the Pentagon used more than 300 of them.

At the same time, the Knight-Ridder News Service reported that the Department of Defense, on the eve of winter, had stopped distributing millions of blankets to homeless programs around the country. The Senate Armed Services Committee had not approved the appropriation. According to the news dispatch, "The Congressional committee said the cost of the blanket program diverted needed money from weaponry."

Thus, our weapons kill people abroad, while homeless people freeze at home.

Are not our moral priorities absurdly distorted?

When I received the message from Dr. Al-Obaidi, I tried to meet his request by reading from his letter on a number of radio interviews in various parts of the country. I have written to him to tell him that. Nothing, of course, can restore his family. All we can do is try to convey to the American public the human consequences of our government's repeated use of violence for political and economic gain. When enough of them see and feel what is happening to people just like us—to families, to children—we may see the beginning of a new movement in this country against militarism and war.

6.

A DIPLOMATIC SOLUTION
May 1999

A friend wrote to ask my opinion on Kosovo. He said many people were turning to him for answers, and he didn't know what to say, so he was turning to me (knowing, I guess, that I always have something to say, right or wrong).

Several things seem clear to me, and they don't fit easily together in a way that points to a clean solution.

Milosevic and his Serb forces are committing atrocities.

But bombing won't help. It can only make things worse, and that is already evident. It is creating more victims, on both sides.

The Kosovo Liberation Army may not represent the wishes of the Kosovar people. It turned to armed struggle to gain independence, ruthlessly putting its countrymen at risk, when a protracted nonviolent campaign of resistance was already going on and should have continued.

I think of South Africa, where a decision to engage in out-and-out armed struggle would have led to a bloody civil war with huge casualties, most of them black. Instead, the African National Congress decided to put up with apartheid longer, but wage a long-term campaign of attrition, with strikes, sabotage, economic sanctions, and international pressure. It worked.

The United States does not have a humanitarian aim in this situation. U.S. foreign policy has never been guided by such concerns, but by political power, economic interest, and sometimes a motive more elusive—machismo. (We want to show the world we are Number One, as president after president has reiterated since the beginning of the Vietnam War.)

The hypocrisy of the Clinton administration is evident after just a glance at recent history. When Chechnya rebelled, demanding independence from Russia just as Kosovo wants it from Yugoslavia now, the Russian army moved in and did terrible things to the people of Chechnya. Clinton did not oppose this. In fact, in fielding one reporter's question, he compared the situation to the American Civil War, when Lincoln would not permit the Confederacy to secede.

There is no sensible military solution to the ethnic cleansing. It could be stopped only by putting in a large ground force, which would mean a full-scale war, which would greatly multiply the present violence.

What is happening to the people of Kosovo is heartrending, and I think the only solution is a diplomatic one, forgetting the treaty the United States tried to force on Serbia. It will take a new agreement, in which the Kosovars will have to settle for some form of autonomy, but no guarantee of independence: a compromise in order to have peace. And the most likely way this diplomatic solution can come about is through the intercession of Russia, which should exercise its influence over the Serbs.

The United States is violating the U.N. Charter. But

any reference to international law may appear futile, since the United States has rendered it worthless for fifty years. The bombing also violates the U.S. Constitution, which requires a declaration of war, and we are certainly waging war.

The United States and NATO (which is the creation of the United States and does its bidding) are floundering, and in the process they are doing enormous damage to human beings. This situation will require the citizens of the NATO countries—especially of the United States—to shout their protest at what is going on, and to demand a diplomatic solution. When a nation issues ultimatums, it leaves no room for compromise and ensures that war will continue.

We learned from Vietnam that the ruthlessness of leaders, the stupidity of "experts," must be countered by the courage, good sense, and persistence of the citizenry.

7.

THEIR ATROCITIES—AND OURS

July 1999

There was a headline recently in my hometown newspaper, the *Boston Globe*: Pentagon Defends Airstrike on Village. U.S. Says Kosovars Were "Human Shields." That brought back the ugliest of memories. It recalled My Lai and other Vietnam massacres, justified by such comments as "the Vietnamese babies are concealing hand grenades."

Here's the logic: Milosevic has committed atrocities; therefore, it is OK for us to commit atrocities. He is terrorizing the Albanians in Kosovo; therefore, we can terrorize the Serbs in Yugoslavia.

I get e-mail messages from Yugoslav opponents of Milosevic, who demonstrated against him in the streets of Belgrade before the air strikes began. They now tell me their children cannot sleep at night, terrified by the incessant bombing. They tell of the loss of light, of water, of the destruction of the basic sources of life for ordinary people.

To Thomas Friedman, columnist for the *New York Times*, all Serbs must be punished, without mercy, because they have "tacitly sanctioned" the deeds of their leaders. That is a novel definition of war guilt. Can we now expect an Iraqi journalist to call for bombs placed in every American supermarket on the grounds that all of us have "tacitly sanctioned" the hundreds of thousands of deaths in Iraq caused by our eight-year embargo?

Official terrorism, whether used abroad or at home, by jet bombers or by the police, always receives an opportunity to explain itself in the press, as ordinary terrorism does not. The thirty-one prisoners and nine guards massacred on orders of New York Governor Nelson Rockefeller in the Attica uprising; the eleven MOVE members, five of whom were children, killed in a fire after their homes were bombed by Philadelphia police; the eighty-six Branch Davidians, including twenty-four children, who died at the Waco compound in an attack ordered by the Clinton administration; the African immigrant murdered by a gang of policemen in New York—all of these events had explanations that, however absurd, are dutifully given time and space in the media.

One of these explanations seeks comfort in relative numbers. We have heard NATO spokesperson Jamie Shea, as well as Clinton, pass off the bombing of Yugoslav civilians by telling us the Serb forces have killed more Albanians than we have killed Serbs—although as the air strikes multiply, the numbers are getting closer. No matter: This math work justifies NATO's killing not just Serbs but Albanian refugees, not just adults but children.

There were those who defended the 1945 firestorm bombing of Dresden (100,000 dead?—we can't be sure) by pointing to the Holocaust. As if one atrocity deserves another! I have heard the deaths of more than 150,000 Japanese citizens in the atomic strikes on Hiroshima and

Nagasaki justified by the terrible acts of the Japanese military in that war.

I suppose if we consider the millions of casualties of all the wars started by national leaders these past sixty years as "tacitly supported" by their populations, some righteous God who made the mistake of reading Thomas Friedman might well annihilate the human race.

The television networks, filling our screen with heartrending photos of the Albanian refugees—and those stories must not be ignored—have not given us a full picture of the human suffering in Yugoslavia. An e-mail came to me, a message from Djordje Vidanovic, a professor of linguistics and semantics at the University of Nis: "The little town of Aleksinac, twenty miles away from my hometown, was hit last night with full force. The local hospital was hit, and a whole street was simply wiped off. What I know for certain is six dead civilians and more than fifty badly hurt. There was no military target around whatsoever."

That was an "accident." As was the bombing of the Chinese Embassy. As was the bombing of a civilian train on a bridge over the Juzna Morava River. As was the bombing of Albanian refugees on a road in southern Kosovo. As was the destruction of a civilian bus with twenty-four dead, including four children.

Some stories come through despite the inordinate attention to NATO propaganda, omnipresent on CNN and other networks (and the shameless Shea announced we bombed a television station in Belgrade because it gives out propaganda).

There was a rare description of the gruesome scene at the bus bombing by Paul Watson of the *Los Angeles Times*.

The *New York Times* reported the demolition of four houses in the town of Merdare by anti-personnel bombs, "killing five people, including Bozina Tosovic, thirty, and his eleven-month-old daughter, Bojana. His wife, six months pregnant, is in the hospital."

Steven Erlanger reported, also in the *New York Times*, that NATO missiles killed at least eleven people in a residential area of Surdulica, a town in southern Serbia. He described "the mounded rubble across narrow Zmaj Jovina Street, where Aleksandar Milic, thirty-seven, died on Tuesday. Mr. Milic's wife, Vesna, thirty-five, also died. So did his mother and his two children, Miljana, fifteen, and Vladimir, eleven—all of them killed about noon when an errant NATO bomb obliterated their new house and the cellar in which they were sheltering."

Are these "accidents," as NATO and U.S. officials solemnly assure us?

One day in 1945 I dropped canisters of napalm on a village in France. I have no idea how many villagers died, but I did not mean to kill them. Can I absolve what I did by calling it "an accident"?

Aerial bombings have as inevitable consequences the killing of civilians, and this is foreseeable, even if the details about who will be the victims cannot be predicted.

The deaths and mutilations caused by the bombing campaign in Yugoslavia are not accidents but the inevitable result of a deliberate and cruel campaign against the people of that country.

There was an extraordinary report by Tim Weiner in the *New York Times* contrasting the scene in Belgrade with that in Washington where the NATO summit was taking place. "In Belgrade . . . Gordana

Ristic, thirty-three, was preparing to spend another night in the basement-cum-bomb-shelter of her apartment building. 'It was a really horrible night last night. There were explosions every few minutes after 2 a.m. . . . I'm sorry that your leaders are not willing to read history.'

"A reporter read to her from Clinton's speeches at the summit meeting. She sounded torn between anger and tears. 'This is the bottom to which civilization, in which I believed, has gone. Clinton is playing a role, singing a song in an opera. It kills me.' As she slept, NATO's leaders dined on soft-shell crabs and spring lamb in the East Room of the White House. Dessert was a little chocolate globe. Jessye Norman sang arias. And as the last limousine left, near midnight, Saturday morning's all-clear sounded in Belgrade."

When I read a few weeks ago that cluster bombs are being used against Yugoslavia and have caused unprecedented amputations in Kosovo hospitals, I felt a special horror. These bombs have hundreds of shrapnel-like metal fragments that enter the body and cannot easily be removed, causing unbearable pain. Serb children have picked up unexploded bombs and been mutilated. I remember being in Hanoi in 1968 and visiting hospitals where children lay in agony, victims of a similar weapon—their bodies full of tiny pellets.

Two sets of atrocities, two campaigns of terrorism—ours and theirs. Both must be condemned. But for that, both must be acknowledged, and if one is given enormous attention, and the other passed over with official, respectful explanations, it becomes impossible to make a balanced moral judgment.

Yes, Milosevic should stand in the dock to answer for war crimes. Clinton, Albright, Cohen, and Clark should stand with him.

There is another factor that we as Americans must consider when we confront the atrocities on both sides. We bear a moral responsibility in any situation to the extent that we have the capacity to affect that situation. In the case of the Milosevic cruelties against the Kosovars, our capacity to intervene—which may have been greater before we rushed to bomb—is very limited, unless we go into a full-scale ground war. If that happens, the resulting tragedy will far exceed the one that has already taken place. But we have a direct responsibility for the cruelties our government inflicts by bombing innocent people in Yugoslavia.

We are seeing liberals and even some radicals, forgetting their own harsh criticism of the controlled press, succumb to the barrage of information about the horrors inflicted on the people of Kosovo. That information is isolated from its context—the human consequences of our bombing campaign, the record of the United States government in ignoring or abetting "ethnic cleansing" in various parts of the world, the refusal of the U.S. and NATO to respond to reasonable and negotiable proposals from the other side. And so those who should know better are led to support violent solutions.

George Seldes, that fierce exposer of the press, and Upton Sinclair, who wrote of the prostitution of the newspapers in *The Brass Check*, both lost their sense of proportion as they were inundated with Allied propaganda in World War I and found themselves supporting a military debacle that ended with ten million dead. Seldes later wrote: "Of the first war years, I will say just this: I made a total fool of myself when I accepted as true the news reports from New York and Europe, which by their volume and repetition overwhelmed what little objective intelligence I had . . . ."

If the Serbian military are killing and expelling the Albanians in Kosovo, it is a reasonable reaction to say: "We must do something." But if that is the only information we are getting, it is a quick and reckless jump to: "We must bomb," or "We must invade." If we don't want to perpetuate the violence on both sides, we will have to demand of our leaders that they discard their macho arrogance ("We will win!" "Milosevic will lose!" "We are the superpower!" "Our credibility is at stake!"). We must demand that they stop bombing and start talking.

There will, at some point, be a negotiated end to the violence in Yugoslavia. But how many people on both sides will have died needlessly and horribly in the interim? That depends on how quickly the American people can raise a powerful cry of protest against the actions of our government.

8.

DELUSION 2000: HOW THE CANDIDATES VIEW THE WORLD
March 2000

Every day, as the soggy rhetoric of the presidential candidates accumulates into an enormous pile of solid waste, we get more and more evidence of the failure of the American political system. The candidates for the job of leader of the most powerful country in the world have nothing important to say. On domestic issues, they offer platitudes about health care and Social Security and taxes, which are meaningless given the record of both political parties. And on foreign policy, utter silence.

That silence is what I want to talk about.

In domestic policy, there are enough slight differences among the candidates to make some liberals and progressives—desperate for hopeful signs—seize upon the most feeble of promises. Al Gore and Bill Bradley take wobbly steps toward covering some fraction of the forty-four million uninsured, but no candidate proposes universal, nonprofit, government-guaranteed health care. John McCain and George W. Bush mutter unintelligibly about one or another tax plan, but no Republican or Democrat talks about taxing the wealth and income of the super-rich in such a way as to make several trillion dollars available for housing, health, jobs, education.

But on foreign and military policy, there are not even mutterings about change. All the candidates vie with one another in presenting themselves as supporters of the Pentagon, desirous of building up our military strength. Here is Mr. Universe—bulging ridiculously with muscles useless for anything except winning contests and bullying the other kids on the block (it is important to be Number One, important to maintain "credibility")—promising to buy more body-building equipment, and asking all of us to pay for it.

How can we, if we have any self-respect, support candidates—Republican or Democrat—who have nothing to say about the fact that the United States, with 4 percent of the world's population, consumes 25 percent of its wealth? How can we support them when they have nothing to say about our obligation to the other 96 percent, many of whom are suffering as a result of American policy?

What is our obligation?

First, to follow the Hippocratic Oath and "Do No Harm." Instead, we are doing much harm.

By depriving the people of Iraq of food, medicine, and vital equipment, we are causing them enormous suffering under the pretense of "sending a message" to Saddam Hussein. It appears we have no other way to send a message but through killing people. How does this differ, except in scale, from the killings done by terrorists around the world, who also defend their acts by claiming their need to "send a message"?

We pretend we care about "democracy" in Cuba—we who have supported dictatorships all over Latin

America for 100 years and in Cuba itself until Fidel Castro came to power. Truth is, we cannot bear the thought that Castro for forty years has defied us, refusing to pay us the homage to which we are accustomed in this hemisphere. Castro has spurned the invitation to become a member of the world capitalist club, and that is, evidently, unforgivable. And so we impose an embargo on Cuba and make its people suffer.

Which candidate, Democrat or Republican, has had the decency to speak out on this embargo, and on the deprivation it has caused for the children of Cuba? What meaning has the phrase "human rights" if people are denied the necessities of life?

Which candidate, Democrat or Republican, has said a word about our obscene possession of thousands of nuclear weapons—while Washington goes into hysterics over the possibility that some country in the Middle East may some day have one nuclear bomb? None of them has the courage to say what common sense tells us, and what someone so expert on military issues and so tied to the Establishment as Paul Nitze (a former arms control adviser in the Reagan Administration) has publicly said: "I see no compelling reason why we should not unilaterally get rid of our nuclear weapons. . . . It is the presence of nuclear weapons that threatens our existence."

While the front pages report the latest solemn pronouncements of the candidates, professing their concern for the well-being of Americans, the inside pages report the brutal Russian assault on Chechnya, with barely a word from these candidates about the well-being of men, women, and children who were huddled in the basements of Grozny, awaiting the next wave of bombings.

There have been a few lame expressions of protest from the Clinton administration, but it is careful not to offend the Russian leaders, and so, last October, the *Toronto Sun* reported: "In Moscow, standing next to her beaming Russian hosts, U.S. Secretary of State Madeleine Albright proclaimed, 'We are opposed to terrorism, meaning Islamic rebels in the Caucasus fighting Russian rule.' We can't forget that Clinton supported the Russian war on Chechnya from 1994 to 1996, going so far (he does get carried away) as to compare Chechnya to the Confederacy of the Civil War, which had to be put down for the sake of the larger nation. Yeltsin as Lincoln—that was a bit of a stretch.

Is it possible that the various candidates—all supported by huge corporate wealth (it is expected that $3 billion will be spent on the elections)—do not dare challenge a foreign policy whose chief motivation is not human rights but business profit?

Behind the coldness to the people of Chechnya and Iraq, there is the crass matter of oil in that part of the world. Last November, Stephen Kinzer of *The New York Times* reported from Istanbul: "Four nations in the Caspian Sea region took a giant step today toward embracing one of President Clinton's cherished foreign policy projects, a pipeline that would assure Western control over the potentially vast oil and natural gas reserves . . . and give the United States greater influence in the region." The word "cherished" suggests an emotional attachment one cannot find with regard to human rights in the Third World. Does Clinton equally "cherish" projects designed to eliminate hunger and illness? Do the presidential candidates?

The World Health Organization has described the plight of ten million people—dying of AIDS or tuberculosis—as "a silent genocide." The numbers make it as serious and frightening as Hitler's genocide, which our political leaders regularly deplore, at no cost to themselves. But no candidate proposes that we stop spending several hundred billions on the military, stop selling arms to countries all over the world, stop the use of land mines, stop training the officers of military dictatorships in the Third World—and use that money to wipe out tuberculosis and stem the spread of AIDS.

Gore, speaking to the U.N. Security Council a few weeks ago, promised to increase the U.S. commitment to fight AIDS up to $325 million. This is a tinier commitment than that of other industrialized countries and less than the money spent for one fighter-bomber. And that sum pales in comparison to the $1.6 billion proposed by the Clinton Administration for Colombia, ostensibly to fight the war on drugs but really to deal with rebellion.

I suppose the problem is that people who are being bombed around the world, or people who are dying as the result of preventable illnesses, do not vote in American elections. Our political system is not sensitive to the needs even of some of our own citizens who don't vote—the homeless, the imprisoned, the very poor—so how can we expect it to care a whit about people 5,000 miles from our voting booths, however miserable their situation? Since our political system—bipartisan in its coldness to human rights—imposes a silence on these issues, it cannot be respected. It can only be protested against, challenged, or, in the words of the Declaration of Independence, referring to a government that has violated its responsibility to its people, "altered or abolished." That's a tall order, but it can be prepared for by a multitude of short steps, in which citizens act, outside of the party system, to redress their grievances.

9.

ONE RADICAL WHO DID IT ALL
April 2000

As the twentieth century came to an end last December, an extraordinary man, whose life spanned the century, died at the age of ninety-seven. His name was Sender Garlin. I first met Sender when he was only eighty-seven years old. It was the fall of 1989, and I had traveled to Boulder to give a talk at the University of Colorado. He was one of the chief organizers of my stay, but I didn't know this longtime radical journalist and pamphleteer, and so I was not prepared for the excitement of my encounter with him.

We met for lunch at the faculty dining room. I assumed this would take an hour, but it lasted for two hours and could have gone on for six, so animated was the conversation, so high the energy, so full of questions was I, so full of the history of this century was Sender Garlin. He kept saying: "It's my turn to question you. Equal time, you know." But I knew we were not equals in what we had to say.

I am a historian, and Sender had lived through some of the most exciting historical moments of our time. He had covered the Moscow purge trials of the 1930s for three left-wing newspapers, the only Western correspondent to be present at all those bizarre proceedings, in which Stalin methodically disposed of his former fellow revolutionaries. In this country, he reported on a different kind of lynching, the trial of the "Scottsboro Boys," nine black youths falsely accused of rape in Alabama during the Depression years and sentenced to death.

He grew up in a working-class environment in Vermont and upstate New York, his father a baker who, according to Sender, was "an equal opportunity employer," enlisting the services "of my mother and my three older brothers."

Reading *The Appeal to Reason* and the writings of Upton Sinclair, Sender at thirteen or fourteen considered himself a socialist.

Covering the bitter labor struggles of the 1920s and 1930s (the textile strike in Gastonia, North Carolina, the turbulent strikes in California as editor of the *Western Worker*), he was deeply affected. Sender Garlin could never be the detached professional journalist, above the battle, any more than John Reed covering the Paterson mill strike of 1913, or Theodore Dreiser writing about the mine struggles in Kentucky.

As a reporter, Sender interviewed Clarence Darrow, Emma Goldman, Lucy Parsons, Huey Long, Lenin's widow Krupskaya, and Olga Kniper-Chekhova, the Moscow theater star and widow of the great Russian writer. Sender helped form the John Reed Club in the early 1930s and was a founding editor of *Partisan Review* before he moved on to write for *The Masses*.

In subsequent visits to Boulder, I got together with Sender whenever I could, and I was reminded each time of his delicious sense of humor, his endless supply of anecdotes. I recall him telling me of his time as a reporter for the *Bronx Home News*, which insisted on a "local angle" in every story, so when Lindbergh flew across the Atlantic, its headline read: "Lindbergh flies over the Bronx on the way to Paris."

But Sender Garlin's main thrust and satirical barbs were always against the system: the exploitation, the racism, the militaristic nationalism that have plagued this century, whether in the extreme form of fascism or in more disguised form.

After moving to Boulder in 1980 with his wife, the poet Martha Millet Garlin, Sender immediately became involved with political activities in the area. He worked energetically with CISPES (Committee in Solidarity with the People of El Salvador) to protest the Reagan administration's policy of sending arms to the death squads there. A colleague of his in CISPES, Gonzalo Santos, hearing of Sender's death, wrote:

"I will miss Sender. He was the greatest role model of an organizer of, and fighter for, the people that I have ever encountered. . . . May he rest in peace for a while, and then shake and straighten things up where he is, even if the Good Lordess Herself has to suffer the sting of his irreverent but true views on heavenly inequities and pomposities. I only hope that as I grow old, I'll be able to emulate such a rich, full life of commitment, activism, intellectual inquiry, joy of life, and loving mentorship to younger generations, as my dear compañero, Sender Garlin, lived."

That speaks for so many of us who knew this remarkable human being.

10.

ARTISTS OF RESISTANCE
July 2001

Whenever I become discouraged (which is on alternate Tuesdays, between three and four) I lift my spirits by remembering: The artists are on our side! I mean those poets and painters, singers and musicians, novelists and playwrights who speak to the world in a way that is impervious to assault because they wage the battle for justice in a sphere which is unreachable by the dullness of ordinary political discourse.

The billionaire mandarins of our culture can show us the horrors of war on a movie screen and pretend they are making an important statement ("War is hell," says the general as he orders his troops forward into no man's land). But the artists go beyond that, to resistance, defiance.

Here is Edna St. Vincent Millay's "Conscientious Objector":

> I shall die, but that is all that I shall do for
>   Death.
> I hear him leading his horse out of the stall; I
>   hear the clatter on the barn-floor.

He is in haste; he has business in Cuba; business in the Balkans,
many calls to make this morning.
But I will not hold the bridle while he cinches
  the girth.
And he may mount by himself: I will not give
  him a leg up.
Though he flick my shoulders with his whip, I
  will not tell him which way the fox ran.
With his hoof on my breast, I will not tell him
  where the black boy hides in the swamp.
I shall die, but that is all that I shall do for
  Death; I am not on his pay-roll.

e.e cummings, whose own experience with the First
World War had powerfully affected him (see his memoir,
The Enormous Room) wrote in the same vein but in his own
unique style:

  i think of Olaf glad and big
  whose warmest heart recoiled at war:
  a conscientious object-or.
  His wellbeloved colonel (trig
  westpointer most succinctly bred)
  took erring Olaf soon in hand.

In that poem, the colonel and other soldiers proceed
to torture Olaf, and cummings wrote:

  Olaf (being to all intents
  a corpse and wanting any rag
  upon what God unto him gave)

responds, without getting annoyed
"I will not kiss your fucking flag."

Langston Hughes, observing the invasion of Ethiopia by Mussolini, wrote simply:

The little fox is still.
The dogs of war have made their kill.

Countee Cullen could also make his point in a few words. Waiting for his fellow writers to speak out on the outrageous framing of the "Scottsboro Boys" in Alabama, he wrote:

Surely, I said,
Now will the poets sing.
But they have raised no cry.
I wonder why.

In *Catch-22*, Joseph Heller created the absurd war resister Yossarian, who at one point, on a bombing run, asks his fellow crewmen: "Do you guys realize, we are going to bomb a city that has no military targets, no railroads, no industries, only people?"

There is a touch, or more, of the anarchist in writers, who (with some shameful exceptions, those who rush to kiss the flag when the trumpets blow) will not go along, even with "good" wars.

Thus, Kurt Vonnegut did not hesitate, in the midst of the self-congratulation that accompanied victory in World War II, to remind the nation of Dresden, our own counterpart, in spades, to the Nazi bombing of London.

His book *Slaughterhouse-Five* held a mirror to our ruthlessness and that of all nations that pretend to moral superiority while joining the enemy in the back and forth of atrocities.

Vonnegut never fails to quote Eugene Debs (a fellow native of Indiana) when Debs, about to go to prison for ten years for opposing World War I, declared to the jury: "While there is a lower class, I am in it; while there is a criminal element, I am of it; while there is a soul in prison, I am not free."

Eugene O'Neill, six months after Pearl Harbor, wrote to his son: "It is like acid always burning in my brain that the stupid butchering of the last war taught men nothing at all, that they sank back listlessly on the warm manure pile of the dead and went to sleep, indifferently bestowing custody of their future, their fate, into the hands of state departments, whose members are trained to be conspirators, card sharks, double-crossers, and secret betrayers of their own people; into the hands of greedy capitalist ruling classes so stupid they could not even see when their own greed began devouring itself; into the hands of that most debased type of pimp, the politician, and that most craven of all lice and job-worshippers, the bureaucrats."

The barrage of films and books glorifying World War II (*The Greatest Generation*, *Saving Private Ryan*, *Flags of Our Fathers*, *Pearl Harbor*, and more) comes at a time when it is necessary for the Establishment to try to wipe out of the public mind the ugly stain of the war in Vietnam, and now that the aura around the Gulf War has turned sour, to forget that too. A justification is needed for the enormous military budget. And so the good war, the best war, is trundled out to give war a good name.

At such a time, our polemical prose is not enough. We need the power of song, of poetry, to remind us of truths deeper than the political slogans of the day.

The years of the war in Vietnam brought forth such music, songs, and lyrics. I'm thinking of Bob Dylan, and his "Masters of War," with his disturbing voice that cannot be duplicated on a printed page, though the words themselves can:

> Come you Masters of War
> You that build the big guns
> You that build the death planes
> You that build the big bombs
> You that hide behind walls
> You that hide behind desks
> I just want you to know
> I can see through your masks.
>
>   *   *   *   *
>
> Let me ask you one question
> Is your money that good?
> Will it buy you forgiveness
> Do you think that it could?
> I think you will find
> When death takes its toll
> All the money you made
> Will never buy back your soul.

The great writers could see through the fog of what was called "patriotism," what was considered "loyalty." Mark Twain, in his brilliant satire *A Connecticut Yankee in King Arthur's Court*, put it this way: "My kind of loyalty was loyalty to one's country, not to its institutions or its office-holders. The country is the real thing, the substantial thing, the eternal thing; it is the thing to watch over, and care for, and be loyal to; institutions are extraneous, they are its mere clothing, and clothing can wear out, become ragged, cease to be comfortable, cease to protect the body from winter, disease, and death. To be loyal to rags, to shout for rags, to worship rags, to die for rags—that is a loyalty of unreason."

George Bernard Shaw, unsure, perhaps, if the message of his plays was clear, stated his philosophy boldly in his prefaces, as in this one from *Major Barbara*: "I am, and have always been, and shall now always be, a revolutionary writer, because our laws make laws impossible; our liberties destroy all freedom; our property is organized robbery; our morality is an impudent hypocrisy . . . our power wielded by cowards and weaklings, and our honor false in all its points. I am an enemy of the existing order."

The great writers of the world have almost always been on the side of the poor, from Dickens to Tolstoy to Balzac to Steinbeck. Percy Bysshe Shelley (whose wife, Mary, was the daughter of the anarchist William Godwin and the feminist Mary Wollstonecraft), in his passionate poem "The Mask of Anarchy," wrote five powerful lines that later, in early twentieth-century United States, would be read aloud to one another by garment workers:

> Rise like Lions after slumber
> In unvanquishable number
> Shake your chains to earth like dew
> Which in sleep had fallen on you—
> Ye are many—they are few.

The social movements of our time have been inspired by Paul Robeson and Pete Seeger, but also by the anonymous voices of the Selma Freedom Chorus.

Today, we have the fierce revolutionary poetry of June Jordan, Alice Walker, and Marge Piercy—all activists as well as poets. And the "slam poetry" of Alix Olson and Aye de Leon. We have the example of a poet in action, the gifted Adrienne Rich, refusing to accept a prize from President Bill Clinton, as her protest against the signing of the "welfare reform" bill.

Arundhati Roy, author of *The God of Small Things*, has joined her energy as a citizen to her brilliance as a novelist in the struggle to save the land and the people of India from the ravages of greedy corporations.

The roster of artists with social consciences is endless. I point to a few to represent so many, because their work, their commitment, encourages and sustains me, and I want it to encourage and sustain others.

11.

OPERATION ENDURING WAR
March 2002

We are "winning the war on terror." I learn this from George Bush's State of the Union Address. "Our progress," he said, "is a tribute to the might of the United States military." My hometown newspaper, the *Boston Globe*, is congratulatory: "On the war front, the Administration has much to take pride in." But the president also tells us that "tens of thousands of trained terrorists are still at large." That hardly suggests we are "winning the war." Furthermore, he says, there is a "grave and growing danger."

Bush singled out Iran, Iraq, and North Korea because they may be building "weapons of mass destruction." And that's not all: "Terror training camps still exist in at least a dozen countries," he says.

The prospect is for a war without end. In no previous administration has any president ever talked about such a war. Indeed, presidents have been anxious to assure the nation that the sacrifices demanded would be finite, and as each war went on, we were told, as in Vietnam, there was "light at the end of the tunnel."

No light is visible in this war on terrorism, for, as the president says, "These enemies view the entire world as a battlefield, and we must pursue them wherever they are."

It seems necessary for the nation to remain frightened. The enemy is everywhere. "The campaign may not be finished on our watch," Bush says. He will pass on the job to the next president, and perhaps the next and the next.

This is an elusive enemy, whose defeat will require an endless war. And so long as the nation is in a state of war, it is possible to demand of the American people certain sacrifices.

Immediately, we must sacrifice our freedoms (although the war is presumably to protect freedom). "We choose freedom and the dignity of every life," the president said. But we cannot choose freedom now. For now, we must give up the freedoms promised by our Bill of Rights.

Thus Congress has passed legislation to give the government sweeping new powers to keep watch over us, enlarging its right to spy with wiretaps and computer surveillance, and allowing officials to conduct secret searches of homes and offices.

The secretary of state can designate any organization as a terrorist organization, and this decision is not subject to review. The USA Patriot Act defines a "domestic terrorist" as someone who violates the law and is engaged in activities that "appear to be intended to . . . influence the policy of government by intimidation or coercion." This could make many activist organizations subject to designation as terrorist organizations. As for noncitizens—and there are twenty million of them in the United States—they can now be subject to indefinite detention and deportation.

So we now have all sorts of enemies to fear—noncitizens and dissidents at home, an infinite number of mysterious enemies abroad. We will have to concentrate not only our resources but our attention on that endless war. We will be looking everywhere in the world for our enemies.

We will not be paying attention to the thousands who die in this country not at the hands of terrorists but because of the profit system, the "free market." When I spoke recently on a radio show in Madison, Wisconsin, a caller asked: Why, grieving as we all should for the thousands of victims of the September 11 action, were we not grieving also for the thousands of people who die on the job, in industrial accidents?

We could extend that question: Why are we not grieving also for the thousands of children who die every year in this country for lack of food and medical care?

The answer seems clear: To do that would call attention not to obscure foreign terrorists but to a system of corporate domination in which profits come before the safety of workers. It would call attention to a political system in which the government can fund hundreds of billions for its military machine but cannot find the money to give free health care, decent housing, minimum family incomes—all those requisites for children to grow up healthy.

It is right to mourn the deaths of 3,000 people who died at the hands of terrorists. But we should also know that every day, according to the U.N. World Food Programme, 11,000 children die of hunger around the world.

The bombs on Afghanistan and the talk of endless war deflect our attention from the millions in Africa, Asia, the Middle East, who die of hunger and disease, victims of a global market system indifferent to human needs.

The World Health Organization, in a report last year entitled "Determinants of Malnutrition," said: "All too frequently, the poor in fertile developing countries stand by watching with empty hands—and empty stomachs—while ample harvests and bumper crops are exported for hard cash. Short-term profits for a few, long-term losses for many. Hunger is a question of maldistribution and inequality, not lack of food."

The economist and Nobel Laureate Amartya Sen has written: "Global capitalism is much more concerned with expanding the domain of market relations than with, say, establishing democracy, expanding elementary education, or enhancing the social opportunities of society's underdogs."

The hundreds of millions of people in the United States and the rest of the world who are without medical care or food or work are the collateral damage of what Pope John Paul II once called "savage, unbridled capitalism." That damage is kept out of sight by the "war on terrorism." The war not only provides huge profits to military contractors and power to the politicians but blocks out the conditions of people's lives, here and abroad.

What shall we do? We start with the core problem: that there is immense wealth available, enough to care for the urgent needs of everyone on Earth, and that this wealth is being monopolized by a small number of individuals, who squander it on luxuries and war while millions die and more millions live in misery. This is a problem understood by people everywhere, because it has a simplicity absent in issues of war and nationalism. That is, they know with supreme clarity—when their attention is not concentrated by the government and the media on waging war—that the world is run by the rich, and that money decides politics, culture, and some of the most intimate human relations.

The evidence for this is piling up, and becoming hard to put aside.

The collapse of the gargantuan Enron Corporation—with its wholesale loss of jobs and the sudden disappearance of health insurance and retirement pensions—points to an economic system that is inherently corrupt.

The sudden impoverishment of Argentina, one of the richest countries in Latin America, provides more evidence. We are seeing the results of "the free market" and "free trade" and the demands for "privatization" in the rules of the World Bank and the International Monetary Fund. Instead of the public taking charge of basic services—water, heat, transportation—private companies took over, and the results were disastrous (as in Bolivia and other countries). In the case of Argentina, a French company took over the water system and quadrupled the fees charged for water.

While criticizing the war on terrorism and exposing its many hypocrisies, we need to realize if we do only that, we too become victims of the war. We too—like so many Americans listening to the president's frightening picture of enemies here, there, everywhere—will have been diverted from an idea that could unite Americans as surely as fear of terrorists.

That idea is a startling one, but immediately recognizable as true: Our most deadly enemies are not in caves and compounds abroad but in the corporate boardrooms and governmental offices where decisions are made that consign millions to death and misery—not deliberately, but as the collateral damage of the lust for profit and power.

It may be an idea whose time has come. We will need the spirit of Seattle and Porto Alegre, a reinvigorated labor movement, a mobilization of people across the rainbow, the beginning of global solidarity, looking to a long-delayed sharing of the fruits of the earth.

12.
WHAT WAR LOOKS LIKE
October 2002

In all the solemn statements by self-important politicians and newspaper columnists about a coming war against Iraq, and even in the troubled comments by some who are opposed to the war, there is something missing. The talk is about strategy and tactics, geopolitics and personalities. It is about air war and ground war, weapons of mass destruction, arms inspections, alliances, oil, and "regime change."

What is missing is what an American war on Iraq will do to tens of thousands or hundreds of thousands of ordinary human beings who are not concerned with geopolitics and military strategy, and who just want their children to live, to grow up. They are not concerned with "national security" but with personal security, with food and shelter and medical care and peace.

I am speaking of those Iraqis and those Americans who will, with absolute certainty, die in such a war, or lose arms or legs, or be blinded. Or they will be stricken with some strange and agonizing sickness that could lead to their bringing deformed children into the world (as happened to families in Vietnam, Iraq, and also the United States).

True, there has been some discussion of American casualties resulting from a land invasion of Iraq. But, as always when the strategists discuss this, the question is not about the wounded and dead as human beings, but about what number of American casualties would result in public withdrawal of support for the war, and what effect this would have on the upcoming elections for Congress and the presidency.

That was uppermost in the mind of Lyndon Johnson, as we have learned from the tapes of his White House conversations. He worried about Americans dying if he escalated the war in Vietnam, but what most concerned him was his political future. If we pull out of Vietnam, he told his friend Senator Richard Russell, "they'll impeach me, won't they?"

In any case, American soldiers killed in war are always a matter of statistics. Individual human beings are missing in the numbers. It is left to the poets and novelists to take us by the shoulders and shake us and ask us to look and listen. In World War I, ten million men died on the battlefield, but we needed John Dos Passos to confront us with what that meant: In his novel *1919*, he writes of the death of John Doe: "In the tarpaper morgue at Châlons-sur-Marne in the reek of chloride of lime and the dead, they picked out the pine box that held all that was left of" him. A few pages later, Dos Passos describes him: "The blood ran into the ground, the brains oozed out of the cracked skull and were licked up by the trenchrats, the belly swelled and raised a generation of bluebottle flies, and the incorruptible skeleton, and the scraps of dried viscera and skin bundled in khaki."

Vietnam was a war that filled our heads with statistics,

of which one stood out, embedded in the stark monument in Washington: 58,000 dead. But one would have to read the letters from soldiers just before they died to turn those statistics into human beings. And for all those not dead but mutilated in some way, the amputees and paraplegics, one would have to read Ron Kovic's account, in his memoir, *Born on the Fourth of July*, of how his spine was shattered and his life transformed.

As for the dead among "the enemy"—that is, those young men, conscripted or cajoled or persuaded to pit their bodies against those of our young men—that has not been a concern of our political leaders, our generals, our newspapers and magazines, our television networks. To this day, most Americans have no idea, or only the vaguest, of how many Vietnamese—soldiers and civilians (actually, a million of each)—died under American bombs and shells.

And for those who know the figures, the men, women, children behind the statistics remained unknown until a picture appeared of a Vietnamese girl running down a road, her skin shredding from napalm, until Americans saw photos of women and children huddled in a trench as GIs poured automatic rifle fire into their bodies.

Ten years ago, in that first war against Iraq, our leaders were proud of the fact that there were only a few hundred American casualties (one wonders if the families of those soldiers would endorse the word "only"). When a reporter asked General Colin Powell if he knew how many Iraqis died in that war, he replied: "That is really not a matter I am terribly interested in." A high Pentagon official told the *Boston Globe*, "To tell you the truth, we're not really focusing on this question."

Americans knew that this nation's casualties were few in the Gulf War, and a combination of government control of the press and the media's meek acceptance of that control ensured that the American people would not be confronted, as they had been in Vietnam, with Iraqi dead and dying.

There were occasional glimpses of the horrors inflicted on the people of Iraq, flashes of truth in the newspapers that quickly disappeared. In mid-February 1991, U.S. planes dropped bombs on an air raid shelter in Baghdad at four in the morning, killing 400 to 500 people—mostly women and children—who were huddled there to escape the incessant bombing. An Associated Press reporter, one of the few allowed to go to the site, said: "Most of the recovered bodies were charred and mutilated beyond recognition."

In the final stage of the Gulf War, American troops engaged in a ground assault on Iraqi positions in Kuwait. As in the air war, they encountered virtually no resistance. With victory certain and the Iraqi army in full flight, U.S. planes kept bombing the retreating soldiers who clogged the highway out of Kuwait City. A reporter called the scene "a blazing hell, a gruesome testament. To the east and west across the sand lay the bodies of those fleeing."

That grisly scene appeared for a moment in the press and then vanished in the exultation of a victorious war, in which politicians of both parties and the press joined. President Bush crowed: "The specter of Vietnam has been buried forever in the desert sands of the Arabian peninsula." The two major news magazines, *Time* and *Newsweek*, printed special editions hailing the victory. Each devoted about a hundred pages to the celebration, mentioning proudly the small number of American casualties. They said not a word about the tens of thousands of Iraqis—soldiers and civilians— themselves victims first of Saddam Hussein's tyranny, and then of George Bush's war.

There was scarcely a photograph of a single dead Iraqi child, or a name of a particular Iraqi, or an image of suffering and grief to convey to the American people what our overwhelming military machine was doing to other human beings.

The bombing of Afghanistan has been treated as if human beings are of little consequence. It has been portrayed as a "war on terrorism," not a war on men, women, children. The few press reports of "accidents" were quickly followed with denials, excuses, justifications. There has been some bandying about of numbers of Afghan civilian deaths—but always numbers. Only rarely has the human story, with names and images, come through as more than a flash of truth, as one day when I read of a ten-year-old boy, named Noor Mohammed, lying on a hospital bed on the Pakistani border, his eyes gone, his hands blown off, a victim of American bombs.

Surely, we must discuss the political issues. We note that an attack on Iraq would be a flagrant violation of international law. We note that the mere possession of dangerous weapons is not grounds for war—else we would have to make war on dozens of countries. We point out that the country that possesses by far the most "weapons of mass destruction" is our country, which has used them more often and with more deadly results than any nation on Earth. We can point to our national history of expansion and aggression. We have powerful evidence of deception and hypocrisy at the highest levels of our government.

But, as we contemplate an American attack on Iraq, should we not go beyond the agendas of the politicians and the experts? (John le Carré has one of his characters say: "I despise experts more than anyone on Earth.")

Should we not ask everyone to stop the high-blown talk for a moment and imagine what war will do to human beings whose faces will not be known to us, whose names will not appear except on some future war memorial?

For this we will need the help of people in the arts, those who through time—from Euripides to Bob Dylan—have written and sung about specific, recognizable victims of war. In 1935, Jean Giraudoux, the French playwright, with the memory of the First World War still in his head, wrote *The Trojan War Will Not Take Place*. Demokos, a Trojan soldier, asks the aged Hecuba to tell him "what war looks like." She responds:

"Like the backside of a baboon. When the baboon is up in a tree, with its hind end facing us, there is the face of war exactly: scarlet, scaly, glazed, framed in a clotted, filthy wig."

If enough Americans could see that, perhaps the war on Iraq would not take place.

13.

OUR JOB IS A SIMPLE ONE: STOP THEM
December 2002

Democracy flies out the window as soon as war comes along. So when officials in Washington talk about democracy, either here or abroad, as they take this country to war, they don't mean it. They don't want democracy; they want to run things themselves. They want to decide whether we go to war. They want to decide the lives and deaths of people in this country, and they certainly want to decide the lives and deaths of people in Iraq and all over the Middle East.

Faced with this attitude, our job is just a simple one: to stop them.

I am not going to go into the Bush arguments, if that's what they are. No, don't make me do that.

Don't make me point out the U.S. violations of international law.

Don't make me point out that even if Saddam Hussein has not gone along with this resolution or that resolution of the U.N. Security Council, the United States is about to violate the fundamental charter of the United Nations, which declares that nations may not initiate wars.

No, don't make me do that.

Don't make me point out how this fear of weapons

of mass destruction does not extend to the United States. Bush officials think if they use that phrase "weapons of mass destruction" again and again and again that people will cower, cower, cower. Never mind that Iraq is a fifth-rate military power and not even the strongest military in the region. Israel, with 200 nuclear weapons, has that distinction. Bush is not demanding that Ariel Sharon rid himself of his weapons of mass destruction or face "regime change."

The media are a pitiful lot. They don't give us any history, they don't give us any analysis, they don't tell us anything. They don't raise the most basic questions: Who has the most weapons of mass destruction in the world by far? Who has used weapons of mass destruction more than any other nation? Who has killed more people in this world with weapons of mass destruction than any other nation? The answer: the United States.

Please, I don't want to hear anything more about Saddam Hussein's possibly making a nuclear bomb in two years, in five years, nobody knows. We have 10,000 nuclear weapons.

No, I don't want to talk about that. It's not worth talking about.

I'd like to make a few general points about war. I was a bombardier in the air force during World War II. I say this not to indicate that I am an expert on war—although, in fact, I am. People who've served in the military, they have a thousand different viewpoints, so nobody can say, "Oh, I served in the military, therefore you have to listen to me." However, in my case . . . I served in the best of wars. The neatest of wars. The war that killed the most people, but for good purpose. The war that had wonderful motives, at least on the part of some people. But that war ended with Hiroshima and Nagasaki and was interspersed with other atrocities committed by the good guys against the bad guys. I, being one of the good guys, feel very proud that I was on the good side, and that if atrocities were to be committed, they were to be committed by good guys. One point: War always has unintended consequences. You start a war, you never know how it ends.

Another point: By now we have reached a point in human history when the means of war have become so horrible that they exceed any possible good that can come out of using them.

Since World War II, war has taken its toll increasingly against civilians. In World War I, there was a ten-to-one ratio of military personnel killed versus civilians, whereas in World War II that ratio got closer to one-to-one. And after World War II, most of the people who have gotten killed in wars have been civilians.

And by the way, I don't want to insist on the distinction—and this is something to think about—between innocent civilians and soldiers who are not innocent. The Iraqi soldiers whom we crushed with bulldozers, toward the end of the Gulf War in 1991, in what way were they not innocent? The U.S. Army just buried them—buried them—hundreds and hundreds and hundreds of them. What of the Iraqi soldiers the United States mowed down in the so-called Turkey Shoot as they were retreating, already defeated? Who were these soldiers on the other side? They weren't Saddam Hussein. They were just poor young men who had been conscripted.

In war you kill the people who are the victims of

the tyrant you claim to be fighting against. That's what you do.

And wars are always wars against children. In every war, unforgivable numbers of children die.

This brings me to the last general point I want to make. We ought to remind our neighbors, remind our friends, remind everybody we can that if we really believe that all people are created equal we cannot go to war.

If we really believe that the children of Iraq have as much a right to live as the children of the United States, then we cannot make war on Iraq.

And if we're going to have globalization, let's have a globalization of human rights. Let's insist that we consider the lives of people in China and Afghanistan and Iraq and Israel and Palestine—that we consider the lives of all these people—equal to one another, and therefore war cannot be tolerated.

14.

A CHORUS AGAINST WAR
March 2003

As I write this it looks like war. This, in spite of the obvious lack of enthusiasm in the country for war. The polls that register "approve" or "disapprove" can only count numbers; they cannot test the depth of feeling. And there are many signs that the support for war is shallow and shaky and ambivalent.

This administration will not likely be stopped, though it knows its support is thin. In fact, that is undoubtedly why it is in such a hurry; it wants to go to war before the support gets any thinner.

The assumption is that once the soldiers are in combat, the American people will unite behind the war. The television screens will show "smart bombs" exploding, and the secretary of defense will assure the American people that civilian casualties are being kept to a minimum. (We're in the age of megadeaths, and any number of casualties less than a million is no cause for concern.)

This is the way it has been. Unity behind the president in time of war. But it may not be that way again.

The anti-war movement will not likely surrender to the martial atmosphere. The hundreds of thousands who marched in Washington and San Francisco and New York and Boston—and in villages, towns, and cities all over the country from Georgia to Montana—will not meekly withdraw. Unlike the shallow support for the war, the opposition to the war is deep and cannot be easily dislodged or frightened into silence.

Indeed, the anti-war feelings are bound to become more intense.

To the demand "Support Our GIs," the movement will be able to reply: "Yes, we support our GIs, we want them to live, we want them to be brought home. The government is not supporting them. It is sending them to die, or to be wounded, or to be poisoned by our own depleted uranium shells."

No, our casualties may not be numerous, but every single one will be a waste of an important human life. We will insist that this government be held responsible for every death, every dismemberment, every case of sickness, every case of psychic trauma caused by the shock of war.

And though the media will be blocked from access to the dead and wounded of Iraq, though the human tragedy unfolding in Iraq will be told in numbers, in abstractions, and not in the stories of real human beings, real children, real mothers and fathers, the movement will find a way to tell that story. And when it does, the American people— who can be cold to death on "the other side," but who also wake up when "the other side" is suddenly seen as a man, a woman, a child, just like us—will respond.

This is not a fantasy, not a vain hope. It happened in the Vietnam years. For a long time, what was being done to the peasants of Vietnam was concealed by statistics, the "body count," without bodies being shown, without faces being shown, without pain, fear, anguish shown. But then the stories began to come through: the story of the My Lai massacre, the stories told by returning GIs of atrocities they had participated in.

And the pictures appeared: the little girl struck by napalm running down the road, her skin shredding, the mothers holding their babies to them in the trenches as GIs poured rounds of bullets from automatic rifles into their bodies.

When those stories began to come out, when the photos were seen, the American people could not fail to be moved. The war "against Communism" was seen as a war against poor peasants in a tiny country half the world away.

At some point in this coming war, and no one can say when, the lies of the administration—"the death of this family was an accident," "we apologize for the dismemberment of this child," "this was an intelligence mistake," "a radar malfunction"—will begin to come apart.

How soon that will happen depends not only on the millions now—whether actively or silently—in the anti-war movement, but also on the emergence of whistle-blowers inside the Establishment who begin to talk, of journalists who become tired of being manipulated by the government and begin to write the truth. And of dissident soldiers sick of a war that is not a war but a massacre: How else to describe the mayhem caused by the most powerful military machine on Earth raining thousands of bombs on a fifth-rate military power already reduced to poverty by two wars and ten years of economic sanctions?

The anti-war movement has the responsibility of encouraging defections from the war machine. It does this simply by its existence, by its example, by its persistence, by its voices reaching out over the walls of government control and speaking to the consciences of people.

Those voices have already become a chorus, joined by Americans in all walks of life, of all ages, in every part of the country.

There is a basic weakness in governments—however massive their armies, however wealthy their treasuries, however they control the information given to the public—because their power depends on the obedience of citizens, of soldiers, of civil servants, of journalists and writers and teachers and artists. When these people begin to suspect they have been deceived, and when they withdraw their support, the government loses its legitimacy, and its power. We have seen this happen in recent decades, all around the globe. Leaders who were apparently all-powerful, surrounded by their generals, suddenly faced the anger of an aroused people, the hundreds of thousands in the streets and the reluctance of the soldiers to fire, and those leaders soon rushed to the airport, carrying their suitcases of money with them.

The process of undermining the legitimacy of our own government has begun. There has been a worm eating at the innards of its complacency all along—the knowledge of the American public, buried, but in a very shallow grave, easy to disinter, that this government came to power by a political coup, not by popular will.

The movement should not let this be forgotten.

The first steps to delegitimize this government are being taken, in small but significant ways.

The wife of the president calls off a gathering of poets in the White House because the poets have rebelled, seeing the march to war as a violation of the most sacred values of poets through the ages.

The generals who led the Gulf War of 1991 speak out against this impending war as foolish, unnecessary, dangerous.

The CIA contradicts the president by saying Saddam Hussein is not likely to use his weapons unless he is attacked.

All across the country—not just the great metropolitan centers, like Chicago, but places like Bozeman, Montana; Des Moines, Iowa; San Luis Obispo, California; Nederland, Colorado; York, Pennsylvania; Gary, Indiana; Carrboro, North Carolina—fifty-seven cities and counties have passed resolutions against the war, responding to their citizens.

The actions will multiply, once the war has begun. The stakes will be higher. People will be dying every day. The responsibility of the peace movement will be huge—to speak to what people may feel but are hesitant to say. To say that this is a war for oil, for business. Bring back the Vietnam-era poster: "War Is Good for Business—Invest Your Son." (In this morning's *Boston Globe*, a headline: "Extra $15 Billion for Military Would Profit New England Firms.")

Yes, by all means, no blood for oil, no blood for Bush, no blood for Rumsfeld or Cheney or Powell. No blood for political ambition, for grandiose designs of empire.

No action should be seen as too small, no nonviolent action should be seen as too large. The calls now for the impeachment of George Bush should multiply. The constitutional requirement "high crimes and misdemeanors" certainly applies to sending our young halfway around the world to kill and be killed in a war of aggression against a people who have not attacked us.

Those poets troubled Laura Bush because by bringing the war into her ceremony they were doing something "inappropriate." That should be the key: People will continue to do "inappropriate" things, because that brings attention—the rejection of propriety, the refusal to be "professional" (which usually means not breaking out of the box your business or your profession insists you stay in).

The absurdity of this war is so starkly clear that people who have never been involved in an anti-war demonstration have been showing up in huge numbers at recent rallies. If you've been to one of them, you can testify to the numbers of young people and older people doing this for the first time.

Arguments for the war are paper thin and fall apart at first touch. Weapons of mass destruction? Iraq may develop one nuclear bomb (though the U.N. inspectors find no sign of development), but Israel has 200 nuclear weapons and the U.S. has 10,000, and six other countries have undisclosed numbers. Saddam Hussein a tyrant? Undoubtedly, like many others in the world. A threat to the world? Then how come the rest of the world, much closer to Iraq, does not want war? Defending ourselves? The most incredible statement of all. Fighting terrorism? No connection found between September 11 and Iraq.

I believe it is the obvious emptiness of the administration position that is responsible for the swift growth of the anti-war movement. And for the emergence of new voices, unheard before, speaking "inappropriately" outside their professional boundaries: 1,500 historians have signed an anti-war petition; businessmen, clergy, have put full-page ads in newspapers. All are refusing to stick to their "profession" and instead are professing that they are human beings first.

I think of Sean Penn traveling to Baghdad, in spite of mutterings about patriotism. Or Jessica Lange and Susan Sarandon and Martin Sheen speaking at anti-war rallies in Washington and New York. Renee Zellweger spoke to a reporter for the *Boston Globe* about "how public opinion is manipulated by what we're told. You see it all the time, especially now! The goodwill of the American people is being manipulated. It gives me the chills. I'm going to go to jail this year!"

Rap artists have been speaking out on war, on injustice. Mr. Lif says: "I think people have been on vacation and it's time to wake up. We need to look at our economic, social, and foreign policies and not be duped into believing the spin that comes from the government and the media."

In the comic strip The Boondocks, which reaches twenty million readers every day, the cartoonist Aaron McGruder has his character, a black youngster named Huey Freeman, say the following: "In this time of war against Osama bin Laden and the oppressive Taliban regime, we are thankful that OUR leader isn't the spoiled son of a powerful politician from a wealthy oil family who is supported by religious fundamentalists, operates through clandestine organizations, has no respect for the democratic electoral process, bombs innocents, and uses war to deny people their civil liberties. Amen."

The voices will multiply. The actions, from silent vigils to acts of civil disobedience (three nuns are facing long jail terms for pouring their blood on missile silos in Colorado), will multiply. If Bush starts a war, he will be responsible for the lives lost, the children crippled, the terrorizing of millions of ordinary people, the American GIs not returning to their families. And all of us will be responsible for bringing that to a halt.

People who have no respect for human life or for freedom or justice have taken over this beautiful country of ours. It will be up to the American people to take it back.

15.

DYING FOR THE GOVERNMENT
March 2003

Our government has declared a military victory in Iraq. As a patriot, I will not celebrate. I will mourn the dead— the American GIs, and also the Iraqi dead, of whom there have been many, many more.

I will mourn the Iraqi children, not just those who are dead, but those who have been blinded, crippled, disfigured, or traumatized. We have not been given in the American media (we would need to read the foreign press) a full picture of the human suffering caused by our bombing.

We got precise figures for the American dead, but not for the Iraqis. Recall Colin Powell after the first Gulf War, when he reported the "small" number of U.S. dead, and when asked about the Iraqi dead, replied: "That is really not a matter I am terribly interested in."

As a patriot, contemplating the dead GIs, I could comfort myself (as, understandably, their families do) with the thought: "They died for their country." But I would be lying to myself.

Those who died in this war did not die for their country. They died for their government. They died for Bush and Cheney and Rumsfeld. And yes, they died for the greed of the oil cartels, for the expansion of the American empire, for the political ambitions of the president. They died to cover up the theft of the nation's wealth to pay for the machines of death.

The distinction between dying for your country and dying for your government is crucial in understanding what I believe to be the definition of patriotism in a democracy. According to the Declaration of Independence—the fundamental document of democracy—governments are artificial creations, established by the people, "deriving their just powers from the consent of the governed," and charged by the people to ensure the equal right of all to "life, liberty, and the pursuit of happiness." Furthermore, as the Declaration says, "whenever any form of government becomes destructive of these ends, it is the right of the people to alter or abolish it."

It is the country that is primary—the people, the ideals of the sanctity of human life and the promotion of liberty. When a government recklessly expends the lives of its young for crass motives of profit and power, always claiming that its motives are pure and moral ("Operation Just Cause" was the invasion of Panama and "Operation Iraqi Freedom" in the present instance), it is violating its promise to the country. War is almost always a breaking of that promise. It does not enable the pursuit of happiness but brings despair and grief.

Mark Twain, having been called a "traitor" for criticizing the U.S. invasion of the Philippines, derided what he called "monarchical patriotism." He said: "The gospel of the monarchical patriotism is: 'The King can do no wrong.' We have adopted it with all its servility, with an unimportant change in the wording: 'Our country, right or wrong!' We have thrown away the most valuable asset we had—the individual's right to oppose both flag and country when he believed them to be in the wrong. We have thrown it away; and with it, all that was really respectable about that grotesque and laughable word, Patriotism."

If patriotism in the best sense (not in the monarchical sense) is loyalty to the principles of democracy, then who was the true patriot, Theodore Roosevelt, who applauded a massacre by American soldiers of 600 Filipino men, women, and children on a remote Philippine island, or Mark Twain, who denounced it?

With the war in Iraq won, shall we revel in American military power and—against the history of modern empires—insist that the American empire will be beneficent?

Our own history shows something different. It begins with what was called, in our high school history classes, "westward expansion"—a euphemism for the annihilation or expulsion of the Indian tribes inhabiting the continent, all in the name of "progress" and "civilization." It continues with the expansion of American power into the Caribbean at the turn of the century, then into the Philippines, and then repeated Marine Corps invasions of Central America and long military occupations of Haiti and the Dominican Republic.

After World War II, Henry Luce, owner of *Time*, *Life*, and *Fortune*, spoke of "the American Century," in which this country would organize the world "as we see fit." Indeed, the expansion of American power continued, too often supporting military dictatorships in Asia, Africa, Latin America, the Middle East, because they were friendly to American corporations and the American government.

The record does not justify confidence in Bush's boast that the United States will bring democracy to Iraq. Should Americans welcome the expansion of the nation's power, with the anger this has generated among so many people in the world? Should we welcome the huge growth of the military budget at the expense of health, education, the needs of children, one fifth of whom grow up in poverty?

I suggest that a patriotic American who cares for his or her country might act on behalf of a different vision. Instead of being feared for our military prowess, we should want to be respected for our dedication to human rights.

Should we not begin to redefine patriotism? We need to expand it beyond that narrow nationalism that has caused so much death and suffering. If national boundaries should not be obstacles to trade—some call it "globalization"—should they also not be obstacles to compassion and generosity?

Should we not begin to consider all children, everywhere, as our own? In that case, war, which in our time is always an assault on children, would be unacceptable as a solution to the problems of the world. Human ingenuity would have to search for other ways.

16.
HUMPTY DUMPTY WILL FALL
August 2003

The "victory" over an already devastated and disarmed Iraq led Bush, Rumsfeld, and their teammates into a locker-room frenzy of exultation and self-congratulation. I half expected to see Bush joyfully pouring beer on Rumsfeld's head and Ashcroft snapping a towel at Ari Fleischer's derrière. But it turns out that the war did not bring order to Iraq, but chaos, not crowds of cheering Iraqis, but widespread hostility. "No to Saddam! No to Bush!" were the signs, as Iraqis contemplated their ruined historic treasures, their destroyed homes, and the graves of their dead—thousands and thousands of civilians and soldiers, with many more men, women, children wounded. And it goes on as I write this in mid-June—an ugly occupation. I see a headline: "U.S. Troops Kill 70 in Iraqi Crackdown."

With each passing day, the Bush administration's lies are being exposed. There were the lies about war being necessary to destroy Iraq's "weapons of mass destruction." But an American army of 200,000, moving aggressively throughout the country, cannot find them. The only weapons of mass destruction in Iraq have been the bombs and missiles raining down by the thousands, the cluster bombs spewing out their deadly pellets, the arsenal of the greatest military power on Earth visiting destruction on a country ruled by a murderous tyrant, but militarily helpless.

There were the lies about wanting "self-determination" for the Iraqis, as the new officialdom, headed by wealthy exiles, was flown into positions of power, just as once Ngo Dinh Diem was flown into Saigon by the United States as Washington proclaimed its intention that Vietnam should govern itself. Through all this there is a sinking feeling that most Americans remain ignorant of these things, and so still support George Bush by a decisive majority.

But consider how volatile is public opinion, how it can change (and has done so many times) with dramatic suddenness. Note the large majority support for George Bush the elder, and then the quick collapse of that support as the glow of victory in the Gulf War faded, and the reality of economic trouble set in.

Think of how in 1965 two-thirds of Americans supported the war in Vietnam, and a few years later two-thirds opposed the war. What happened in between? A gradual realization of having been lied to, an osmosis of the truth, of information seeping more and more through the cracks of the propaganda system. That is beginning to happen now.

A bit of historical perspective reminds us that governments that seem to be in total control—of guns, of money, of the minds of the population—find that all their power is futile against the power of an aroused citizenry. The leaders awake one morning to see a million angry people in the streets of the capital city, and they begin packing their bags and calling for a helicopter. This is not a fantasy but history. It's the history of the Philippines, Indonesia, Russia, of East Germany, Poland, Hungary, Rumania, and other places where change looked hopeless and then it happened.

Throughout history, imperial powers, gloating over victories, become overextended and overconfident, as their citizens begin to get uneasy because their day-to-day fundamental needs are being sacrificed for military glory while their young are sent to die in wars. The uneasiness grows and grows, and the citizenry gather in resistance in larger and larger numbers, and one day the top-heavy empire falls over.

We don't expect Bush to scurry off in a helicopter. But he can lose the next election, just as he lost the last one, and this time perhaps not all the king's judges or all the king's men will be able to put Humpty Dumpty together again.

And there are already people around the country calling for his impeachment. Of course, we do not expect a craven Congress to impeach him. They were willing to impeach Nixon for breaking into a building. They will not impeach Bush for breaking into a country. They were willing to impeach Clinton because of his sexual shenanigans, but they will not impeach Bush for his pandering to the super-rich. Still, it is good to bring up impeachment, because the Constitution allows it for "high crimes and misdemeanors," and it is an opportunity to discuss the high crimes of this government.

The change in public opinion starts with a low-level discontent, at first vague, with no connection being made to the policies of the government. And then, as some connections become unmistakable, indignation rises, and people begin to speak out, to organize, to act. Today, all over the country, there is a growing awareness of the shortage of teachers, of nurses, of medical care, of affordable housing, of cuts in human services in every state of the union. A teacher writes a letter to the *Boston Globe*: "I may be one of 600 Boston teachers who will be laid off as a result of budget shortfalls." And the teacher connects it to the billions spent for bombs "sending innocent Iraqi children to hospitals in Baghdad."

Rebellion often starts in the culture, which we are seeing today—the poets in defiance, the actors and writers speaking out, the musicians and rap groups taking a stand—a rebellion that is first ignored by the major media, and then becomes hard to ignore. We see Michael Moore winning an Academy Award and speaking his mind to a huge national and international audience. We see the radical collective Def Poetry Jam winning a Tony Award as millions watch.

The arrogance, the posturing of this administration, is becoming more and more hollow as its lies become exposed, its "victory" in Iraq a sham, its tax program an obvious theft by the rich.

The rest of the planet (and remember, we in the United States are only 4 percent of the world population) views this nation not as a liberator but as a marauder. After the unprecedented worldwide demonstrations of more than ten million people against the invasion of Iraq, a *New York Times* reporter wrote: "There are two superpowers, the United States and world public opinion."

In Aeschylus's play *The Persians*, now running in

New York, we see the fall of another seemingly invincible empire. The chorus recognizes a new reality:

> *All those years we spent jubilant,*
> *seeing the trifling, cowering*
> *world from the height of our*
> *shining saddles, brawling our might*
> *across the earth as we forged an*
> *empire, I never questioned . . .*
> *It seemed so clear—our fate was to rule.*
> *That's what I thought at the time.*
> *But perhaps we were merely*
> *deafened for years by the din*
> *of our own empire-building,*
> *the shouts of battle,*
> *the clanging of swords,*
> *the cries of victory.*

Those of us who become momentarily disheartened by "the cries of victory" should remind ourselves of that long history in which seemingly insurmountable power fell not only of its own unbearable weight, but also because of the resistance of those who refused finally to bear that weight, and would not give up.

17.

AN OCCUPIED COUNTRY

October 2003

It has become clear, very quickly, that Iraq is not a liberated country, but an occupied country. We became familiar with the term "occupied country" during World War II. We talked of German-occupied France, German-occupied Europe. And after the war we spoke of Soviet-occupied Hungary, Czechoslovakia, Eastern Europe. It was the Nazis, the Soviets, who occupied other countries. Now we are the occupiers. True, we liberated Iraq from Saddam Hussein, but not from us. Just as in 1898 we liberated Cuba from Spain, but not from us. Spanish tyranny was overthrown, but the United States established a military base in Cuba, as we are doing in Iraq. U.S. corporations moved in to Cuba, just as Bechtel and Halliburton and the oil corporations are moving into Iraq. The United States was deciding what kind of constitution Cuba would have, just as our government is now forming a constitution for Iraq. Not a liberation, an occupation.

And it is an ugly occupation. On August 7, the *New York Times* reported that U.S. General Ricardo Sanchez in Baghdad was worried about Iraqi reaction to the occupation. Iraqi leaders who were pro-American were giving him a message, as he put it: "When you take a father in front of his family and put a bag over his head and put him on the ground you have had a significant adverse effect on his dignity and respect in the eyes of his family." (That's very perceptive.)

CBS News reported on July 19 that Amnesty International is looking into a number of cases of suspected torture in Iraq by American authorities. One such case involves Khraisan al-Aballi, CBS said. "When American soldiers raided the al-Aballi house, they came in shooting. . . . They shot and wounded his brother Dureid." U.S. soldiers took Khraisan, his 80-year-old father, and his brother away. "Khraisan says his interrogators stripped him naked and kept him awake for more than a week, either standing or on his knees, bound hand and foot, with a bag over his head," CBS reported. Khraisan told CBS he informed his captors, "I don't know what you want. I don't know what you want. I have nothing." At one point, "I asked them to kill me," Khraisan said. After eight days, they let him and his father go. Paul Bremer, the U.S. administrator of Iraq, responded, "We are, in fact, carrying out our international obligations."

On June 17, two reporters for the Knight Ridder chain wrote about the Fallujah area: "In dozens of interviews during the past five days, most residents across the area said there was no Ba'athist or Sunni conspiracy against U.S. soldiers, there were only people ready to fight because their relatives had been hurt or killed, or they themselves had been humiliated by home searches and road stops." One woman said, after her husband was taken from their home because of empty wooden crates, which they had bought for firewood, that the United States is guilty of terrorism. "If I find any American soldiers, I will cut their heads off," she said. According to the reporters, "Residents in At Agilia—a village north of Baghdad—said two of their farmers and five others from another village were killed when U.S. soldiers shot them while they were watering their fields of sunflowers, tomatoes, and cucumbers."

Soldiers who are set down in a country where they were told they would be welcomed as liberators only to find they are surrounded by a hostile population become fearful, trigger-happy, and unhappy. We've been reading the reports of GIs angry at their being kept in Iraq. In mid-July, an ABC News reporter in Iraq told of being pulled aside by a sergeant who said to him: "I've got my own 'Most Wanted List.'" He was referring to the deck of cards the U.S. government published, featuring Saddam Hussein, his sons, and other wanted members of the former Iraqi regime. "The aces in my deck are Paul Bremer, Donald Rumsfeld, George Bush, and Paul Wolfowitz," the sergeant said.

Such sentiments are becoming known to the American public. In May, a Gallup Poll reported that only 13 percent of the American public thought the war was going badly. By July 4, the figure was 42 percent. By late August, it was 49 percent.

Then there is the occupation of the United States. I wake up in the morning, read the newspaper, and feel that we are an occupied country, that some alien group has taken over. Those Mexican workers trying to cross the border—dying in the attempt to evade immigration officials (ironically, trying to cross into land taken from Mexico by the United States in 1848)—those Mexican workers are not alien to me. Those millions of people in this country who are not citizens and therefore, by the Patriot Act, are subject to being pulled out of their homes and held indefinitely by the FBI, with no constitutional rights—those people are not alien to me. But this small group of men who have taken power in Washington, they are alien to me. I wake up thinking this country is in the grip of a president who was not elected, who has surrounded himself with thugs in suits who care nothing about human life abroad or here, who care nothing about freedom abroad or here, who care nothing about what happens to the earth, the water, the air. And I wonder what kind of world our children and grandchildren will inherit. More Americans are beginning to feel, like the soldiers in Iraq, that something is terribly wrong, that this is not what we want our country to be.

More and more every day, the lies are being exposed. And then there is the largest lie: that everything the United States does is to be pardoned because we are engaged in a "war on terrorism." This ignores the fact that war is itself terrorism, that the barging into people's homes and taking away family members and subjecting them to torture, that is terrorism, that invading and bombing other countries does not give us more security but less security.

You get some sense of what this government means by the "war on terrorism" when you examine what Rumsfeld said a year ago when he was addressing the NATO ministers in Brussels. "There are things that we know," he said. "And then there are known unknowns. That is to say, there are things that we now know that we don't know. But there are also unknown unknowns. There are things we do not know we don't know. . . . That is, the absence of evidence is not evidence of absence. . . . Simply because you do not have evidence that something exists does not mean that you have evidence that it doesn't exist."

Well, Rumsfeld has clarified things for us.

That explains why this government, not knowing exactly where to find the criminals of September 11, will just go ahead and invade and bomb Afghanistan, killing thousands of people, driving hundreds of thousands from their homes, and still not know where the criminals are.

That explains why the government, not really knowing what weapons Saddam Hussein is hiding, will invade and bomb Iraq, to the horror of most of the world, killing thousands of civilians and soldiers and terrorizing the population.

That explains why the government, not knowing who are terrorists and who are not, will put hundreds of people in confinement at Guantanamo under such conditions that twenty have tried to commit suicide.

That explains why, not knowing which noncitizens are terrorists, the attorney general will take away the constitutional rights of twenty million of them.

The so-called war on terrorism is not only a war on innocent people in other countries, but it is also a war on the people of the United States: a war on our liberties, a war on our standard of living. The wealth of the country is being stolen from the people and handed over to the super-rich. The lives of our young are being stolen. And the thieves are in the White House.

It's interesting to me that polls taken among African Americans have shown consistently 60 percent opposition to the war in Iraq. Shortly after Colin Powell made his report to the United Nations on "Weapons of Mass

Destruction," I did a phone interview with an African American radio station in Washington, D.C., a program called *GW on the Hill*. After I talked with the host there were eight call-ins. I took notes on what the callers said: John: "What Powell said was political garbage."

Another caller: "Powell was just playing the game. That's what happens when people get into high office."

Robert: "If we go to war, innocent people will die for no good reason."

Kareen: "What Powell said was hogwash. War will not be good for this country."

Susan: "What is so good about being a powerful country?"

Terry: "It's all about oil."

Another caller: "The U.S. is in search of an empire and it will fall as the Romans did. Remember when Ali fought Foreman. He seemed asleep but when he woke up he was ferocious. So will the people wake up."

It is often said that this administration can get away with war because unlike Vietnam, the casualties are few. True, only a few hundred battle casualties, unlike Vietnam. But battle casualties are not all. When wars end, the casualties keep mounting up—sickness, trauma. After the Vietnam War, veterans reported birth defects in their families due to the Agent Orange spraying in Vietnam. In the first Gulf War there were only a few hundred battle casualties, but the Veterans Administration reported recently that in the ten years following the Gulf War, 8,000 veterans died. About 200,000 of the 600,000 veterans of the Gulf War filed complaints about illnesses incurred from the weapons our government used in the war. In the current war, how many young men and women sent by Bush to liberate Iraq will come home with related illnesses?

What is our job? To point all this out.

Human beings do not naturally support violence and terror. They do so only when they believe their lives or country are at stake. These were not at stake in the Iraq War. Bush lied to the American people about Saddam and his weapons. And when people learn the truth—as happened in the course of the Vietnam War—they will turn against the government. We who are for peace have the support of the rest of the world. The United States cannot indefinitely ignore the ten million people who protested around the world on February 15. The power of government—whatever weapons it possesses, whatever money it has at its disposal—is fragile. When it loses its legitimacy in the eyes of its people, its days are numbered. We need to engage in whatever nonviolent actions appeal to us. There is no act too small, no act too bold. The history of social change is the history of millions of actions, small and large, coming together at critical points to create a power that governments cannot suppress. We find ourselves today at one of those critical points.

18

THE LOGIC OF WITHDRAWAL
January 2004

A note of explanation: In the spring of 1967, my book Vietnam: The Logic of Withdrawal *was published by Beacon Press. It was the first book on the war to call for immediate withdrawal, no conditions. Many liberals were saying: "Yes, we should leave Vietnam, but President Johnson can't just do it; it would be very hard to explain to the American people." My response, in the last chapter of my book, was to write a speech for Lyndon Johnson, explaining to the American people why he was ordering the immediate evacuation of American armed forces from Vietnam. No, Johnson did not make that speech, and the war went on. But I am undaunted, and willing to make my second attempt at speech writing. This time, I am writing a speech for whichever candidate emerges as Democratic Party nominee for president. My supposition is that the nation is ready for an all-out challenge to the Bush administration, for its war policy and its assault on the well-being of the American people. And only such a forthright, courageous approach to the nation can win the election and save us from another four years of an administration that is reckless with American lives and American values.*

My fellow Americans, I ask for your vote for president because I believe we are at a point in the history of our country where we have a serious decision to make. That decision will deeply affect not only our lives, but also the lives of our children and grandchildren. At this moment in our nation's history, we are on a very dangerous course. We can remain on that course, or we can turn onto a bold new path to fulfill the promise of the Declaration of Independence, which guarantees everyone an equal right to life, liberty, and the pursuit of happiness.

The danger we are in today is that the war—a war without any foreseeable end—is not only taking the lives of our young but exhausting the great wealth of our nation. That wealth could be used to create prosperity for every American but is now being squandered on military interventions abroad that have nothing to do with making us more secure.

We should listen carefully to the men serving in this war.

Tim Predmore is a five-year veteran of the army. He is just finishing his tour of duty in Iraq. He writes: "We have all faced death in Iraq without reason or justification. How many more must die? How many more tears must be shed before Americans awake and demand the return of the men and women whose job it is to protect them rather than their leader's interest?"

What is national security? This administration defines national security as sending our young men and women around the world to wage war on country after country—none of them strong enough to threaten us. I define national security as making sure every American has health care, employment, decent housing, a clean environment. I define national security as taking care of our people who are losing jobs, taking care of our senior citizens, taking care of our children.

Our current military budget is $400 billion a year, the largest in our history, larger even than when we were in the Cold War with the Soviet Union. And now we will be spending an additional $87 billion for the war in Iraq. At the same time, we are told that the government has cut funds for health care, education, the environment, and even school lunches for children. Most shocking of all is the cut, in billions of dollars, for veterans' benefits.

If I became president, I would immediately begin to use the great wealth of our nation to provide those things, which represent true security.

Immediately on taking office, I would propose to Congress, and use all my power to ensure that this legislation passes, that we institute a brand-new health care system, one that builds on the success of our Medicare program, and that has been used effectively in other countries in the world.

I would call it Health Security, because it would guarantee to every man, woman, and child free medical care, including prescription drugs, paid for out of the general treasury, like the free medical care for members of Congress, and for members of our armed services. This would save billions of dollars wasted today in administrative costs, profits for insurance companies and pharmaceutical firms, huge salaries for CEOs of private medical plans. There would be no paperwork for the patient, and no worries about whether any medical condition, any medical emergency, would be covered. No worry that losing your job would mean an end to your medical insurance.

I would do something else immediately on taking office. I would ask Congress for a Full Employment Act, guaranteeing jobs to anyone who is willing to work. We would give the private sector all the opportunity to provide work, but where it fails to do so, the government would become the employer of last resort. We would use as a model the great social programs of the New Deal, when millions of people were given jobs after the private sector had failed to do so.

I would also take steps to reverse the attacks on our environment by the Bush administration, which has been more concerned for the profits of large corporations than for the air, land, and water we depend on. In December of 2002, it relaxed its pollution standards for antiquated coal-fired power plants in the Midwest, and those emissions cause hundreds of premature deaths each year. It has refused to sign the Kyoto agreement on global warming, though climate change is an enormous peril to the coming generations. The Nuclear Regulatory Agency in January of 2003 refused to order a nuclear reactor closed though its lid had rusted nearly all the way through, because, according to an internal commission report, the agency did not want to impose unnecessary costs on the owner and was reluctant to give the industry a black eye.

This administration has done nothing to stop the emissions from the chemical plants all over the country, and it has stored chemical weapons in areas where residents have become sick as a result. In April of 2003, Darline Stephens of Anniston, Alabama, told a journalist: "I live five or ten miles from chemical weapons. We're over there searching for weapons of mass destruction in Iraq, but we have them here in our hometown."

The Bush presidency has sacrificed the cause of clean air and clean water because it has ties to the automobile industry, the oil industry, the chemical industry, and other great commercial enterprises. I would insist on regulating those industries in order to save the environment for us, our children, our grandchildren.

A decision must be made, and I promise to make it. We cannot have Health Security, or job security, or a decent environment, unless we decide we will no longer be a nation that sends its military everywhere in the world against nations that pose no threat to us. We have already lost 400 lives in Iraq. Over 2,000 of our young have been wounded, some of them so seriously that the word "wounded" does not convey the reality.

Robert Acosta is twenty years old. He has lost his right hand and part of his forearm.

Twenty-one-year-old Edward Platt has had his leg amputated above the knee.

The entertainer Cher, visiting the Walter Reed Hospital in Washington, called in to a television program, saying, "As I walked into the hospital the first person I ran into was a boy about nineteen or twenty years old who'd lost both of his arms. . . . And when I walked into the hospital and visited all these boys all day long . . . everyone had lost either one arm . . . or two limbs. . . . I just think that if there was no reason for this war, this was the most heinous thing I'd ever seen. . . . I go all over the world and I must say that the news we get in America has nothing to do with the news that you get outside of this country."

The families of those who have died in this war are asking questions which this administration cannot answer. I read recently about the mother of Captain Tristan Aitken, who was thirty-one years old, and died in combat in Iraq. She said about her son: "He was doing his job. He had no choice, and I'm proud of who he was. But it makes me mad that this whole war was sold to the American public and to the soldiers as something it wasn't. Our forces have been convinced that Iraqis were responsible for September 11, and that's not true."

This mother has it right. Americans were led into war, being told again and again by the highest officials of government, including the president, that it was absolutely necessary. But we now know that we were deceived. We were told that Iraq had weapons of mass destruction that were a danger to us and the world. These weapons, despite enormous efforts by both an international team and our own government's investigative body, have not been found.

Virtually every nation in the world, and public opinion all over the planet, believed we should not go to war. Countries much closer to Iraq than ours did not feel threatened, so why should the United States—with its enormous arsenal of nuclear weapons and with its warships on every sea—have felt threatened?

Common sense should have told us that Iraq, devastated by two wars (first with Iran, then with our country) and then ruined by ten years of economic sanctions, could not be a threat sufficient to justify war. But that common sense did not exist in Washington, either in the White House, which demanded war, or in Congress, which rushed to approve war. We now know that decision was wrong and that the president of the United States and the people around him were not telling us the truth.

As a result of believing the president, we went to war in violation of the U.N. Charter, in defiance of public opinion all over the world, and thus in a single move placed ourselves outside the family of nations and destroyed the goodwill that so many people everywhere had toward our country.

On September 11, 2001, a terrorist attack in New York and Washington took close to 3,000 lives. The Bush administration has used that tragic event as an excuse to go to war, first in Afghanistan and now in Iraq. But neither war has made us safer from terrorism. The Bush administration lied to the American people about a connection between Iraq and Al Qaeda, when even the CIA has not been able to find such a connection.

Indeed, by its killing of thousands of people in both countries, the Bush administration has inflamed millions of people in the Middle East against us and increased the ranks of the terrorists.

The Iraqi people are happy to be rid of Saddam Hussein, but now they want to be rid of us. They do not want our military to occupy their country. If we believe in self-determination, in the freedom of the Iraqis to choose their own way of life, we should listen to their pleas, leave their country, and allow them to work out their own affairs.

I would, therefore, as president, call for an orderly withdrawal of our troops from Iraq and Afghanistan. I would remove our troops from elsewhere in the Middle East. Only the oil interests benefit from that military presence.

I am proposing a fundamental change in the foreign policy of our country. This administration believes that we, as the most powerful nation in the world, should use that power to establish military bases all over the world, to control the oil of the Middle East, to determine the destinies of other countries.

I believe that we should use our great power not for military purposes but to bring food and medicine to those areas of the world that have been devastated by war, by disease, by hunger. If we took a fraction of our military budget we could combat malaria, tuberculosis, and AIDS. We could provide clean water for the billion people in the world who don't have it and would save millions of lives. That would be an accomplishment we could be proud of. But how proud can we be of military victories over weak nations, in which we overthrow dictators but at the same time bomb and kill the people who are the victims of these dictators? And the tyrants we overthrow are very often the ones we have helped stay in power, like the Taliban in Afghanistan or Saddam Hussein in Iraq.

We are at a turning point in the history of our nation. We can go on being a great military power, engaging in war after war, in which innocent people abroad and our own men and women die or are crippled for life. Or we can become a peaceful nation, always ready to defend ourselves, but not sending our troops and planes all over the world for the benefit of the oil interests and the other great corporations that profit from war.

We can choose to use the wealth of our nation and the talents of our people for war, or we can use that wealth and talent to better the lives of men, women, and children in this country. We can continue being the target of anger and terrorism and indignation by the rest of the world, or we can be a model of what a good society should be like, peaceful in the world, prosperous at home.

The choice will come in the ballot box. I ask you to choose for the peace of the world, and the security of the American people.

19.
OPPOSING THE WAR PARTY
May 2004

The *Progressive* has been a thorn in the side of the Establishment for almost a hundred years. Its life span covers two world wars and six smaller wars. It saw the fake prosperity of the 1920s and the tumult of the 1930s. Its voice remained alive through the Cold War and the hysteria over communism.

Through all that, down to the present day, and the wars against Afghanistan and Iraq, this intrepid magazine has been part of the long struggle for peace, for a boundary-less world. It may be useful to recall some of the heroes—some famous, some obscure—of that historic resistance to war.

When the United States government in 1917 decided to send its young men into the slaughterhouse of the First World War, one of the few voices in Washington speaking out against this was a senator from Wisconsin. This was Robert La Follette, founder of the *Progressive*, who wrote in the June 1917 issue:

"Every nation has its war party. It is not the party of democracy. It is the party of autocracy. It seeks to dominate absolutely. It is commercial, imperialistic, ruthless. It tolerates no opposition. It is just as arrogant, just as despotic, in London, or in Washington, as in Berlin. The American Jingo is twin to the German Junker. . . . If there is no sufficient reason for war, the war party will make war on one pretext, then invent another."

The Socialist Party, with its hundreds of thousands of supporters, opposed the war, calling it "a crime against the people of the United States." The nation had been at war for a year when the Socialist leader Eugene Debs spoke in Canton, Ohio, outside a prison where three Socialists were serving time for opposing the draft. Debs said: "They tell us that we live in a great free republic; that our institutions are democratic; that we are a free and self-governing people. That is too much, even for a joke. . . . Wars throughout history have been waged for conquest and plunder. . . . And that is war in a nutshell. The master class has always declared the wars; the subject class has always fought the battles."

Those last words were quoted by Supreme Court Justice Oliver Wendell Holmes in writing the court's unanimous decision that Debs had violated the Espionage Act because his words, with draft-age youngsters in the crowd, "would obstruct the recruiting or enlistment service." Debs was sentenced to ten years in prison. Before sentencing him, the judge, acting in the tradition of a judicial system obsequious to the war-making branches of government, denounced those who, like Debs, "would strike the sword from the hand of this nation while she is engaged in defending herself against a foreign and brutal power."

Here's what the *Progressive* had to say about Holmes's decision: It is "a doctrine quite unsuitable to a free country."

Helen Keller, a persistent voice against militarism and a contributor to the *Progressive*, also reacted to the Supreme Court's decision on Eugene Debs. She wrote an open letter to Debs: "I write because my heart cries out, and will not be still. I write because I want you to know that I should be proud if the Supreme Court convicted me of abhorring war, and doing all in my power to oppose it. When I think of the millions who have suffered in all the wicked wars of the past, I am shaken with the anguish of a great impatience. I want to fling myself against all brute powers that destroy life and break the spirit of man."

Despite the huge propaganda campaign of the government and the obedience of the press (the *New York Times* asked its readers "to communicate to proper authorities any evidence of sedition"), there was widespread resistance. About 900 people were imprisoned for speaking against the war, and 65,000 men declared themselves conscientious objectors.

In Oklahoma, the Socialist Party and the IWW formed a "Working Class Union" and planned a draft resisters' march on Washington. There, 450 members of the union were arrested and sentenced to prison. In Boston, 8,000 marched against the war. The draft had been instituted because men were not responding to the call to enlist. But ultimately more than 330,000 were classified as draft evaders.

The first woman in the House of Representatives, Jeannette Rankin of Montana, was asked to speak for "the womanhood of the country" in supporting the war. Instead she said during the roll call: "I want to stand by my country, but I cannot vote for war. I vote No." A few months earlier, in the pages of the *Progressive*, Belle Case

La Follette had saluted Rankin by noting how frequently suffragists were asked, derisively, "How about women holding office?" Explained La Follette: "The average objector to women's suffrage generally puts this question to an advocate with the finality of playing a trump card." No longer, she wrote. Rankin had won the respect of her colleagues. "Liberal minded, sympathetic, trained in economics, her attitude on public questions represents the progressive and enlightened twentieth century spirit," said Belle Case La Follette. (Two decades later, when Congress was voting for war again, Jeannette Rankin was the one vote against it. Today, there is a thriving peace movement in Montana, which invokes her name as it demonstrates against the intervention in Iraq.)

When the leaders of the IWW were put on trial for their activities against the First World War, one of them spoke to the court:

"You ask me why the IWW is not patriotic for the United States. If you were a bum without a blanket . . . if your job had never kept you long enough in a place to qualify you to vote; if every person who represented law and order and the nation beat you up, railroaded you to jail, and the good Christian people cheered and told them to go to it, how in hell do you expect a man to be patriotic? This is a businessman's war, and we don't see why we should go out and get shot in order to save the lovely state of affairs that we now enjoy."

World War II was the "good war," because it was fought against Hitler and the evils of fascism. But its goodness was put into question by the massive bombing of civilians in Germany and Japan, culminating in the atrocities of the firebombing of Tokyo and the nuclear bombs that annihilated about 200,000 in Hiroshima and Nagasaki.

At home, the war did not look as glorious to black people suffering segregation and humiliation. A black journalist wrote: "The Negro . . . is angry, resentful, and utterly apathetic about the war. 'Fight for what?' he is asking. 'This war doesn't mean a thing to me. If we win, I lose, so what?' "

Here in the *Progressive*, six months after Pearl Harbor, Milton Mayer warned that war was corrupting the nation, that we were condemning all Germans, all Japanese, that racism and jingoism were on the rise. "Here we are, with our tiny bit of hard-won humanness hanging now by a thread, and we are trying to teach our people to hate. A little German girl, a relative of mine and a refugee, went into a store and heard the jukebox singing something about 'Slap the Dirty Jap.' She screamed. In the Germany that to her is horror, the jukeboxes played a ballad called 'Slap the Dirty Jew.' "

Early in the Vietnam War, before the Gulf of Tonkin and the rapid escalation, there was an editorial in the *Progressive*: "The tragedy of our role in Vietnam is but the current installment of an old story. Our commitment to 'stop Communism' too often leads us to support corrupt and decadent regimes detested by the peoples of those countries."

That was a minority voice in the country in 1963, but the movement against the war soon began to grow. Some of the first to speak out were the most vulnerable to punishment—young blacks in the South. In McComb, Mississippi, in mid-1965, young blacks who had just learned that a classmate had been killed in Vietnam distributed a leaflet: "No Mississippi Negroes should be fighting in Viet Nam for the White man's freedom until all the Negro People are free in Mississippi." (the *Progressive*, by the way, was not AWOL on civil rights. "You were born into a society which spelled out with brutal clarity and in as many ways as possible that you were a worthless human being," James Baldwin wrote here in his "Letter to My Nephew.")

One of the most famous figures in the world, the heavyweight champion of the world, Muhammad Ali, refused to serve in what he called a "white man's war." His boxing title was taken away from him, but he stood fast.

Martin Luther King Jr., against the advice of other black leaders, spoke out in 1967 at the Riverside Church in New York: "Somehow this madness must cease. We must stop now. I speak as a child of God and brother to the suffering poor of Vietnam. I speak for those whose land is being laid waste, whose homes are being destroyed, whose culture is being subverted. I speak for the poor of America. . . . I speak as a citizen of the world."

This was the greatest movement against war in the nation's history. On October 15, 1969, perhaps two million people across the nation gathered not only in the big cities, but in towns and villages that had never seen an anti-war demonstration.

Priests, nuns, lay people invaded draft boards and seized draft records to express their opposition to what the government was doing. The priest and poet Daniel Berrigan, on the occasion of one of the first of these draft board actions in Maryland by the "Catonsville Nine," wrote a "Meditation:" "Our apologies, good friends, for the fracture of good order, the burning of paper instead of children, the angering of the orderlies in the front parlor of the charnel house. We could not, so help us God, do otherwise. . . . The time is past when good men can remain silent, when obedience can segregate men from public risk, when the poor can die without defense."

Fifteen years later, his brother Philip Berrigan echoed those words while protesting against the nuclear arms race. "The law is the Grand Illusion," he wrote in 1983 in the *Progressive*. "It is not law at all, but anti-law. With endless pretension, it legitimates every phase of nuclear execution. Cloaked in probity, it stuns the mind and paralyzes the will, turning conscience to cowardice, protest to acquiescence. . . . We should break the anti-law, nonviolently, lovingly, responsibly. We should break it and fill the jails, for the only way out of nuclear imprisonment is into jail."

When the United States government went to war against Iraq in 1991, the longtime editor of the *Progressive* Erwin Knoll wrote: "I believe in ingenious, nonviolent struggle for justice and against oppression. So I won't support our troops—not in the Persian Gulf or anywhere else. And I won't support anyone else's troops when they go about their murderous business."

Knoll spoke out against "a cycle of human violence that must be stopped because there is no such thing as a just war. Never was. Never will be."

The spirit of La Follette, of Debs, of Helen Keller, of Martin Luther King Jr., of Daniel and Philip Berrigan and Erwin Knoll lives on today in the millions of Americans who oppose the present war in Iraq: those who hold vigil and demonstrate every day, every week, in towns and cities all over the country, the Military

Families Against the War, the Families for Peaceful Tomorrows, the young people who have learned from the past and continue the struggle for peace.

The challenge remains. On the other side are formidable forces: money, political power, the major media. On our side are the people of the world. On our side also is a power greater than money or weapons: the truth.

20.

WHAT DO WE DO NOW?
June 2004

It seems very hard for some people—especially those in high places, but also those striving for high places—to grasp a simple truth: The United States does not belong in Iraq. It is not our country. Our presence is causing death, suffering, destruction, and so large sections of the population are rising against us. Our military is then reacting by bombing and shooting and rounding up people simply on suspicion. Amnesty International, a year after the invasion, reported: "Scores of unarmed people have been killed due to excessive or unnecessary use of lethal force by coalition forces during public demonstrations, at checkpoints, and in house raids. Thousands of people have been detained [estimates range from 8,500 to 15,000], often under harsh conditions, and subjected to prolonged and often unacknowledged detention. Many have been tortured or ill-treated, and some have died in custody."

The initial battles in Fallujah brought this report from Amnesty International: "Half of at least 600 people who died in the recent fighting between Coalition forces and insurgents in Fallujah are said to have been civilians, many of them women and children."

In light of this, any discussion of "What do we do now?" must start with the understanding that the present U.S. military occupation is morally unacceptable.

The suggestion that we simply withdraw from Iraq is met with laments: "We mustn't cut and run. . . . We must stay the course. . . . Our reputation will be ruined." That is exactly what we heard when, at the start of the Vietnam escalation, some of us called for immediate withdrawal. The result of staying the course was 58,000 Americans and three million Vietnamese dead.

"We can't leave a vacuum there." I think it was John Kerry who said that. What arrogance to think that when the United States leaves a place there's nothing there! The same kind of thinking saw the enormous expanse of the American West as "empty territory" waiting for us to occupy it, when hundreds of thousands of Indians lived there already.

The history of military occupations of Third World countries is that they bring neither democracy nor security. The long U.S. occupation of the Philippines, following a bloody war in which American troops finally subdued the Filipino independence movement, did not lead to democracy but rather to a succession of dictatorships, ending with Ferdinand Marcos. The long U.S. occupations of Haiti (1915–1934) and the Dominican Republic (1916–1924) led only to military rule and corruption in both countries.

The only rational argument for continuing on the present course is that things will be worse if we leave. There will be chaos, there will be civil war, we are told. In Vietnam, supporters of the war promised a bloodbath if U.S. troops withdrew. That did not happen. There is a history of dire forecasts for what will happen if we desist from deadly force. If we did not drop the bomb on Hiroshima, it was said, we would have to invade Japan and huge casualties would follow. We know now, and knew then, that was not true. (The United States had broken the Japanese code and had intercepted the cables from Tokyo to the emissary in Moscow, which made clear that the Japanese were ready to surrender so long as the position of the Emperor was secure.)

Truth is, no one knows what will happen if the United States withdraws. We face a choice between the certainty of mayhem if we stay and the uncertainty of what will follow if we leave.

There is a possibility of reducing that uncertainty by replacing a U.S. military presence with an international nonmilitary presence. It is conceivable that the United Nations could arrange, as U.S. forces leave, for a multinational team of peacekeepers and negotiators, including, importantly, people from the Arab countries. Such a group might bring together Shiites, Sunnis, and Kurds, and work out a solution for self-governance, which would give all three groups a share in political power.

Simultaneously, the United Nation should arrange for shipments of food and medicine, from the United States and other countries, as well as a corps of engineers to begin the reconstruction of the country.

In a situation that is obviously bad and getting worse, some see the solution in enlarging the military presence. The right-wing columnist David Brooks wrote in mid-April: "I never thought it would be this bad," but he then expressed his joy that President Bush is "acknowledging the need for more troops." This fits the definition of fanaticism: When you find you're going in the wrong direction, you double your speed.

John Kerry echoes that fanaticism. If he learned anything from his experience in Vietnam, he has forgotten it. There, too, repeated failure to win the support of the Vietnamese people led to sending more and more troops into Tennyson's "valley of death."

In a recent piece in the *Washington Post*, Kerry talks about "success" in military terms. "If our military commanders request more troops we should deploy them." He seems to think that if we "internationalize" our disastrous policy, it becomes less of a disaster. "We also need to renew our effort to attract international support in the form of boots on the ground to create a climate of security in Iraq." Is that what brings security—"boots on the ground"?

Kerry writes: "We should urge NATO to create a new out-of-area operation for Iraq under the lead of a U.S. commander. This would help us obtain more troops from major powers." More troops, more troops. And the United States must be in charge—that old notion that the world can trust our leadership—despite our long record of moral failure.

To those who worry about what will happen in Iraq after our troops leave, they should consider the effect of having foreign troops stay: continued, escalating bloodshed, continued insecurity, increased hatred for the United States in the entire Muslim world of over a billion people, and increased hostility everywhere. The effect of that will be the exact opposite of what our political leaders—of both parties—claim they intend to achieve, a "victory" over terrorism. When you inflame the anger of an entire population, you have enlarged the breeding ground for terrorism.

What of the other long-term effects of continued occupation? I'm thinking of the poisoning of the moral fiber of our soldiers—being forced to kill, maim, imprison innocent people, becoming the pawns of an imperial power after they were deceived into believing they were fighting for freedom, democracy, against tyranny. I'm thinking of the irony that those very things we said our soldiers were dying for—giving their eyes, their limbs for—are being lost at home by this brutal war. Our freedom of speech is diminished, our electoral system corrupted, congressional and judicial checks on executive power nonexistent. And the costs of the war—the $400 billion military budget (which Kerry refuses to consider lowering)—make it inevitable that people in this country will suffer from lack of health care, a deteriorating school system, dirtier air and water.

Kerry does not seem to understand that he is giving away his strongest card against Bush—the growing disillusion with the war among the American public. He thinks he is being clever by saying he will wage the war better than Bush. But by declaring his continued support for the military occupation, he is climbing aboard a sinking ship.

We do not need another war president. We need a peace president. And those of us in this country who feel this way should make our desire known in the strongest of ways to the man who may be our next occupant of the White House.

21.

OUR WAR ON TERRORISM
November 2004

I am calling it "our" war on terrorism because I want to distinguish it from Bush's war on terrorism, and from Sharon's, and from Putin's. What their wars have in common is that they are based on an enormous deception: persuading the people of their countries that you can deal with terrorism by war. These rulers say you can end our fear of terrorism—of sudden, deadly, vicious attacks, a fear new to Americans—by drawing an enormous circle around an area of the world where terrorists come from (Afghanistan, Palestine, Chechnya) or can be claimed to be connected with (Iraq), and by sending in tanks and planes to bomb and terrorize whoever lives within that circle. Since war is itself the most extreme form of terrorism, a war on terrorism is profoundly self-contradictory. Is it strange, or normal, that no major political figure has pointed this out?

Even within their limited definition of terrorism, they—the governments of the United States, Israel, Russia—are clearly failing. As I write this, three years after the events of September 11, the death toll for American servicemen has surpassed 1,000, more than 150 Russian children have died in a terrorist takeover of a school, Afghanistan is in chaos, and the number of significant terrorist attacks rose to a twenty-one-year high in 2003, according to official State Department figures. The highly respected International Institute for Strategic Studies in London has reported that "over 18,000 potential terrorists are at large with recruitment accelerating on account of Iraq."

With the failure so obvious, and the president tripping over his words trying to pretend otherwise (August 30: "I don't think you can win" and the next day: "Make no mistake about it, we are winning"), it astonishes us that the polls show a majority of Americans believing the president has done "a good job" in the war on terrorism.

I can think of two reasons for this.

First, the press and television have not played the role of gadflies, of whistleblowers, the role that the press should play in a society whose fundamental doctrine of democracy (see the Declaration of Independence) is that you must not give blind trust to the government. They have not made clear to the public—I mean vividly, dramatically clear—what have been the human consequences of the war in Iraq.

I am speaking not only of the deaths and mutilations of American youth, but the deaths and mutilations of Iraqi children. (I am reading at this moment of an American bombing of houses in the city of Fallujah, leaving four children dead, with the U.S. military saying this was part of a "precision strike" on "a building frequently used by terrorists.") I believe that the American people's natural compassion would come to the fore if they truly understood that we are terrorizing other people by our "war on terror."

154

A second reason that so many people accept Bush's leadership is that no counterargument has come from the opposition party. John Kerry has not challenged Bush's definition of terrorism. He has not been forthright. He has dodged and feinted, saying that Bush has waged "the wrong war, in the wrong place, at the wrong time." Is there a right war, a right place, a right time? Kerry has not spoken clearly, boldly, in such a way as to appeal to the common sense of the American people, at least half of whom have turned against the war, with many more looking for the wise words that a true leader provides. He has not clearly challenged the fundamental premise of the Bush administration: that the massive violence of war is the proper response to the kind of terrorist attack that took place on September 11, 2001.

Let us begin by recognizing that terrorist acts—the killing of innocent people to achieve some desired goal—are morally unacceptable and must be repudiated and opposed by anyone claiming to care about human rights. The September 11 attacks, the suicide bombings in Israel, the taking of hostages by Chechen nationalists—all are outside the bounds of any ethical principles.

This must be emphasized, because as soon as you suggest that it is important, to consider something other than violent retaliation, you are accused of sympathizing with the terrorists. It is a cheap way of ending a discussion without examining intelligent alternatives to present policy.

Then the question becomes: What is the appropriate way to respond to such awful acts? The answer so far, given by Bush, Sharon, and Putin, is military action. We have enough evidence now to tell us that this does not stop terrorism, may indeed provoke more terrorism, and at the same time leads to the deaths of hundreds, even thousands, of innocent people who happen to live in the vicinity of suspected terrorists.

What can account for the fact that these obviously ineffective, even counterproductive, responses have been supported by the people of Russia, Israel, the United States? It's not hard to figure that out. It is fear, a deep, paralyzing fear, a dread so profound that one's normal rational faculties are distorted, and so people rush to embrace policies that have only one thing in their favor: They make you feel that something is being done. In the absence of an alternative, in the presence of a policy vacuum, filling that vacuum with a decisive act becomes acceptable.

And when the opposition party, the opposition presidential candidate, can offer nothing to fill that policy vacuum, the public feels it has no choice but to go along with what is being done. It is emotionally satisfying, even if rational thought suggests it does not work and cannot work.

If John Kerry cannot offer an alternative to war, then it is the responsibility of citizens, with every possible resource they can muster, to present such an alternative to the American public.

Yes, we can try to guard in every possible way against future attacks, by trying to secure airports, seaports, railroads, other centers of transportation. Yes, we can try to capture known terrorists. But neither of those actions can bring an end to terrorism, which comes from the fact that millions of people in the Middle East and elsewhere are angered by American policies, and out of these millions come those who will carry their anger to fanatic extremes.

The CIA senior terrorism analyst who has written a book signed "Anonymous" has said bluntly that U.S. policies—supporting Sharon, making war on Afghanistan and Iraq—"are completing the radicalization of the Islamic world."

Unless we reexamine our policies—our quartering of soldiers in a hundred countries (the quartering of foreign soldiers, remember, was one of the grievances of the American revolutionaries), our support of the occupation of Palestinian lands, our insistence on controlling the oil of the Middle East—we will always live in fear. If we were to announce that we will reconsider those policies, and began to change them, we might start to dry up the huge reservoir of hatred where terrorists are hatched.

Whoever the next president will be, it is up to the American people to demand that he begin a bold reconsideration of the role our country should play in the world. That is the only possible solution to a future of never-ending, pervasive fear. That would be "our" war on terrorism.

22.

HARNESS THAT ANGER
January 2005

In the days after the election, it seemed that all my friends were either depressed or angry, frustrated or indignant, or simply disgusted. Neighbors who had never said more than hi to me stopped me on the street and delivered passionate little speeches that made me think they had just listened to a rebroadcast of H. G. Wells's *The War of the Worlds*, in which powerful creatures arrive on Earth to take it over.

But then I reconsidered: They had not been listening to H. G. Wells. There really were strange and powerful creatures that had just occupied the United States and now wanted to take over the rest of the world. Yes, Bush was reelected president, and whether there was fraud in the voting process or not, John Kerry quickly threw in the towel. The minnow called for reconciliation with the crocodile.

The reelected Bush triumphantly announced that he had the approval of the nation to carry out his agenda. There came no sign of opposition from what was supposed to be the opposition party. In short, the members of the club, after a brief skirmish on the campaign trail (costing a total of a billion dollars or so) were back having drinks at the same bar. When, in mid-November, the presidential library of Bill Clinton opened, former presidents, Democratic and Republican, along with the current president, sat side by side and declared their fervent desire for unity.

But someone was left out of the celebration, this insistence that we were all one happy family, accepting the president for another four years. The American people were not quite in agreement.

Consider this: Bush won 51 percent of a voting population that was just 60 percent of the eligible voters. That means Bush won the approval of 31 percent of the eligible voters. Kerry won 28 percent of the eligible voters.

The 40 percent who did not cast a ballot seemed to be saying there was no candidate they could approve of. I suspect that a large percentage of those who voted had the same feeling, but voted anyway. Is this a decisive victory? Has the will of the people been followed? (If we were truly democratic, then maybe the 40 percent nonvoters who were the plurality might have their wish: no president at all.)

The president may insist he has "a mandate," but it is up to the rest of us to declare firmly that he doesn't. Sure, he had more votes than his Democratic opponent, but, to most of the electorate, that candidate did not represent a real choice. More than half the public, in opinion polls over the past six months, had declared their opposition to the war. Neither major party candidate represented their view, so they were effectively disenfranchised.

What to do now? Harness those fierce emotions reacting to the election. In that anger, disappointment, grieving frustration there is enormous combustible energy, which, if mobilized, could reinvigorate an anti-war movement that had been slowed by the all-consuming election campaign. It is in the nature of election campaigns to siphon off the vitality of people imbued with a heartfelt cause, dilute that cause, and pour it into the dubious endeavor to propel one somewhat better candidate into office. But with the election over, there is no more need to hold back, to do as too many well-meaning people did, which was to follow uncritically in the footsteps of a candidate who dodged and squirmed on almost every major issue.

Freed from the sordid confines of our undemocratic political process, we can now turn all our energies to do what is discouraged by the voting system—to speak boldly and clearly about what must be done to turn our country around.

And let's not worry about offending that 22 percent of the country (we don't know the exact number, but it is certainly a minority) who are religious and political fundamentalists, who invoke God in the service of mass murder and imperial conquest, who ignore the biblical injunctions to love one's neighbor, to beat swords into plowshares, to care for the poor and downtrodden.

Most Americans do not want war.

Most want the wealth of this country to be used for human needs—health, work, schools, children, decent housing, a clean environment—rather than for billion-dollar nuclear submarines and four billion-dollar aircraft carriers.

They can be deflected from their most human beliefs by a barrage of government propaganda, dutifully repeated by television and talk radio and the major newspapers.

But this is a temporary phenomenon, and as people begin to sense what is happening, their natural instinct for empathy with other human beings emerges.

We saw this in the Vietnam years, when at first two-thirds of the nation, trusting the government and given no reason for skepticism by a subservient press, supported the war. A few years later, when the reality of what we were doing in Vietnam began to show itself—when the body bags piled up here, and the images of napalmed children in Vietnam appeared on TV screens, and the horror of the My Lai massacre, at first ignored, finally surfaced—the nation turned against the war.

The reality of what is going on in Iraq is more and more coming through the smoke of government propaganda and media timidity. It cannot help but touch the hearts of the people of this country, as they see our soldiers going innocently into Iraq, but becoming brutalized by the war, practicing torture on helpless prisoners, shooting the wounded, bombing houses and mosques, turning cities into rubble, and driving families out of their homes into the countryside.

As I write this, the city of Fallujah has been turned into rubble by a ferocious bombing campaign. Photos are beginning to appear (though not yet in the major media, so cowardly are they) of children with limbs gone, an infant lying on a cot, one leg missing. It is the classic story of a military power possessing the latest, most deadly of weapons, trying to subdue the hostile population of a small, weak country by sheer cruelty, which only increases the resistance. The war in Fallujah cannot be won. It should not be won.

The movement here against the war must confront

the horror of the situation by a variety of bold actions. We will take up the classic instruments of citizens in the history of social movements: demonstrations (there will be a big one in Washington on Inauguration Day), vigils, picket lines, parades, occupations, acts of civil disobedience.

We will be appealing to the good conscience of the American people.

We will be asking questions:

What kind of country do we want to live in?

Do we want to be reviled by the rest of the world?

Do we have a right to invade and bomb other countries, pretending we are saving them from tyranny and in the process killing them in huge numbers? (What is the death toll so far in Iraq? 30,000? 100,000?)

Do we have a right to occupy a country when the people of that country obviously do not want us there?

Election results deceive us by registering the half-hearted, diluted beliefs of a population forced to reduce its true desires to the narrow dimensions of a voting booth. But we are not alone, not in this country, certainly not in the world. (Let's not forget that 96 percent of Earth's population resides outside our borders.) We do not have to do the job alone. Social movements have always had a powerful ally: the inexorable reality that operates in the world impervious to the aims of those who rule their countries. That reality is operating now. The "war on terror" is turning into a nightmare. Whistleblowers from the administration itself are beginning to reveal secrets. (A high CIA official writes of "imperial hubris" and then leaves the agency.) Soldiers are questioning their mission. The corruption attending the war—the billion-dollar contracts to Halliburton and Bechtel—is coming into the open.

The Bush administration, riding high and arrogant, adhering to the rule of the fanatic, which is to double your speed when you are going in the wrong direction, will find itself going over a cliff, too late to stop.

If the leaders of the Democratic Party do not understand this reality, do not squarely address the desires of people in every part of the country (forget the red, the blue, the nonsensical generalizations that ignore the complexities of human thought), they will find themselves tailgating the Bush vehicle as it heads for disaster.

Will the Democratic Party, so craven and unreliable, face a revolt from below which will transform it?

Or will it give way (four years from now? eight years from now?) to a new political movement that honestly declares its adherence to peace and justice?

Sooner or later, profound change will come to this nation tired of war, tired of seeing its wealth squandered, while the basic needs of families are not met. These needs are not hard to describe. Some are very practical, some are requirements of the soul: health care, work, living wages, a sense of dignity, a feeling of being at one with our fellow human beings on Earth.

The people of this country have their own mandate.

23.
CHANGING MINDS, ONE AT A TIME
March 2005

As I write this, the day after the inauguration, the banner headline in the *New York Times* reads: "BUSH, AT 2ND INAUGURAL, SAYS SPREAD OF LIBERTY IS THE 'CALLING OF OUR TIME.'"

Two days earlier, on an inside page of the *Times*, was a photo of a little girl, crouching, covered with blood, weeping. The caption read: "An Iraqi girl screamed yesterday after her parents were killed when American soldiers fired on their car when it failed to stop, despite warning shots, in Tal Afar, Iraq. The military is investigating the incident."

Today, there is a large photo in the *Times* of young people cheering the president as his entourage moves down Pennsylvania Avenue. They do not look very different from the young people shown in another part of the paper, along another part of Pennsylvania Avenue, protesting the inauguration.

I doubt that those young people cheering Bush saw the photo of the little girl. And even if they did, would it occur to them to juxtapose that photo to the words of George Bush about spreading liberty around the world?

That question leads me to a larger one, which I

suspect most of us have pondered: What does it take to bring a turnaround in social consciousness—from being a racist to being in favor of racial equality, from being in favor of Bush's tax program to being against it, from being in favor of the war in Iraq to being against it? We desperately want an answer, because we know that the future of the human race depends on a radical change in social consciousness.

It seems to me that we need not engage in some fancy psychological experiment to learn the answer, but rather to look at ourselves and to talk with our friends. We then see, though it is unsettling, that we were not born critical of existing society. There was a moment in our lives (or a month, or a year) when certain facts appeared before us, startled us, and then caused us to question beliefs that were strongly fixed in our consciousness—embedded there by years of family prejudices, orthodox schooling, imbibing of newspapers, radio, and television.

This would seem to lead to a simple conclusion: that we all have an enormous responsibility to bring to the attention of others information they do not have, which has the potential of causing them to rethink long-held ideas. It is so simple a thought that it is easily overlooked as we search, desperate in the face of war and apparently immovable power in ruthless hands, for some magical formula, some secret strategy to bring peace and justice to the land and to the world.

"What can I do?" The question is thrust at me again and again as if I possessed some mysterious solution unknown to others. The odd thing is that the question may be posed by someone sitting in an audience of a thousand people, whose very presence there is an instance of information being imparted, which, if passed on, could have dramatic consequences. The answer then is as obvious and profound as the Buddhist mantra that says: "Look for the truth exactly on the spot where you stand."

Yes, thinking of the young people holding up the pro-Bush signs at the inauguration, there are those who will not be budged by new information. They will be shown the bloodied little girl whose parents have been killed by an American weapon, and find all sorts of reasons to dismiss it: "Accidents happen. . . . This was an aberration. . . . It is an unfortunate price of liberating a nation," and so on.

There is a hard core of people in the United States who will not be moved, whatever facts you present, from their conviction that this nation means only to do good, and almost always does good, in the world, that it is the beacon of liberty and freedom (words used forty-two times in Bush's inauguration speech). But that core is a minority, as is that core of people who carried signs of protest at the inauguration.

In between those two minorities stand a huge number of Americans who have been brought up to believe in the beneficence of our nation, who find it hard to believe otherwise, but who can rethink their beliefs when presented with information new to them.

Is that not the history of social movements?

There was a hard core of people in this country who believed in the institution of slavery. Between the 1830s, when a tiny group of abolitionists began their agitation, and the 1850s, when disobedience of the fugitive slave acts reached their height, the Northern public, at first ready to do violence to the agitators, now embraced their cause.

What happened in those years? The reality of slavery, its cruelty, as well as the heroism of its resisters, was made evident to Americans through the speeches and writings of the abolitionists, the testimony of escaped slaves, the presence of magnificent black witnesses like Frederick Douglass and Harriet Tubman. Something similar happened during those years of the Southern black movement, starting with the Montgomery Bus Boycott, the sit-ins, the Freedom Rides, the marches. White people—not only in the North, but also in the South—were startled into an awareness of the long history of humiliation of millions of people who had been invisible and who now demanded their rights.

When the Vietnam War began, two-thirds of the American public supported the war. A few years later, two-thirds opposed the war. While some remained adamantly pro-war, one-third of the population had learned things that overthrew previously held ideas about the essential goodness of the American intervention in Vietnam. The human consequences of the fierce bombing campaigns, the "search and destroy" missions, became clear in the image of the naked young girl, her skin shredded by napalm, running down a road; the women and children huddled in the trenches in My Lai with soldiers pouring rifle fire onto them; marines setting fire to peasant huts while the occupants stood by, weeping.

Those images made it impossible for most Americans to believe President Johnson when he said we were fighting for the freedom of the Vietnamese people, that it was all worthwhile because it was part of the worldwide struggle against communism.

In his inauguration speech, and indeed, through all

four years of his presidency, George Bush has insisted that our violence in Afghanistan and Iraq has been in the interest of freedom and democracy, and essential to the "war on terrorism." When the war on Iraq began almost two years ago, about three-fourths of Americans supported the war. Today, the public opinion polls show that at least half of the citizenry believes it was wrong to go to war.

What has happened in these two years is clear: a steady erosion of support for the war, as the public has become more and more aware that the Iraqi people, who were supposed to greet the U.S. troops with flowers, are overwhelmingly opposed to the occupation. Despite the reluctance of the major media to show the frightful toll of the war on Iraqi men, women, children, or to show U.S. soldiers with amputated limbs, enough of those images have broken through, joined by the grimly rising death toll, to have an effect.

But there is still a large pool of Americans, beyond the hard-core minority who will not be dissuaded by any facts (and it would be a waste of energy to make them the object of our attention), who are open to change. For them, it would be important to measure Bush's grandiose inaugural talk about the "spread of liberty" against the historical record of American expansion. It is a challenge not just for the teachers of the young to give them information they will not get in the standard textbooks, but for everyone else who has an opportunity to speak to friends and neighbors and work associates, to write letters to newspapers, to call in on talk shows.

The history is powerful: the story of the lies and massacres that accompanied our national expansion, first across the continent victimizing Native Americans, then overseas as we left death and destruction in our wake in Cuba, Puerto Rico, Hawaii, and especially the Philippines. The long occupations of Haiti and the Dominican Republic, the repeated dispatch of marines into Central America, the deaths of millions of Koreans and Vietnamese, none of them resulting in democracy and liberty for those people.

Add to all that the toll of the American young, especially the poor, black and white, a toll measured not only by the corpses and the amputated limbs, but the damaged minds and corrupted sensibilities that result from war.

Those truths make their way, against all obstacles, and break down the credibility of the warmakers, juxtaposing what reality teaches against the rhetoric of inaugural addresses and White House briefings. The work of a movement is to enhance that learning, make clear the disconnect between the rhetoric of "liberty" and the photo of a bloodied little girl weeping.

And also to go beyond the depiction of past and present, and suggest an alternative to the paths of greed and violence. All through history, people working for change have been inspired by visions of a different world. It is possible, here in the United States, to point to our enormous wealth and suggest how, once not wasted on war or siphoned off to the super-rich, that wealth can make possible a truly just society.

The juxtapositions wait to be made. The recent disaster in Asia, alongside the millions dying of AIDS in Africa, next to the $500 billion military budget, cry out for justice. The words of people from all over the world gathered year after year in Porto Alegre, Brazil, and other places—"a new world is possible"—point to a time when national boundaries are erased, when the natural riches of the world are used for everyone.

The false promises of the rich and powerful about "spreading liberty" can be fulfilled, not by them, but by the concerted effort of us all, as the truth comes out, and our numbers grow.

24.
AFTER THE WAR
January 2006

The war against Iraq, the assault on its people, the occupation of its cities, will come to an end, sooner or later. The process has already begun. The first signs of mutiny are appearing in Congress. The first editorials calling for withdrawal from Iraq are beginning to appear in the press. The anti-war movement has been growing, slowly but persistently, all over the country. Public opinion polls now show the country decisively against the war and the Bush administration. The harsh realities have become visible. The troops will have to come home.

And while we work with increased determination to make this happen, should we not think beyond this war? Should we begin to think, even before this shameful war is over, about ending our addiction to massive violence and instead using the enormous wealth of our country for human needs? That is, should we begin to speak about ending war—not just this war or that war, but war itself? Perhaps the time has come to bring an end to war, and turn the human race onto a path of health and healing.

A group of internationally known figures, celebrated both for their talent and their dedication to human rights (Gino Strada, Paul Farmer, Kurt Vonnegut, Nadine

173

Gordimer, Eduardo Galeano, and others), will soon launch a worldwide campaign to enlist tens of millions of people in a movement for the renunciation of war, hoping to reach the point where governments, facing popular resistance, will find it difficult or impossible to wage war.

There is a persistent argument against such a possibility, which I have heard from people on all parts of the political spectrum: We will never do away with war because it comes out of human nature. The most compelling counter to that claim is in history: We don't find people spontaneously rushing to make war on others. What we find, rather, is that governments must make the most strenuous efforts to mobilize populations for war. They must entice soldiers with promises of money, education, must hold out to young people whose chances in life look very poor that here is an opportunity to attain respect and status. And if those enticements don't work, governments must use coercion: They must conscript young people, force them into military service, threaten them with prison if they do not comply. Furthermore, the government must persuade young people and their families that though the soldier may die, though he or she may lose arms or legs, or become blind, that it is all for a noble cause, for God, for country.

When you look at the endless series of wars of this century you do not find a public demanding war, but rather resisting it, until citizens are bombarded with exhortations that appeal, not to a killer instinct, but to a desire to do good, to spread democracy or liberty or overthrow a tyrant.

Woodrow Wilson found a citizenry so reluctant to enter the First World War that he had to pummel the nation with propaganda and imprison dissenters in order to get the country to join the butchery going on in Europe.

In the Second World War, there was indeed a strong moral imperative, which still resonates among most people in this country and which maintains the reputation of World War II as "the good war." There was a need to defeat the monstrosity of fascism. It was that belief that drove me to enlist in the Air Force and fly bombing missions over Europe. Only after the war did I begin to question the purity of the moral crusade. Dropping bombs from five miles high, I had seen no human beings, heard no screams, seen no children dismembered. But now I had to think about Hiroshima and Nagasaki, and the firebombings of Tokyo and Dresden, the deaths of 600,000 civilians in Japan, and a similar number in Germany.

I came to a conclusion about the psychology of myself and other warriors: Once we decided, at the start, that our side was the good side and the other side was evil, once we had made that simple and simplistic calculation, we did not have to think anymore. Then we could commit unspeakable crimes and it was all right.

I began to think about the motives of the Western powers and Stalinist Russia and wondered if they cared as much about fascism as about retaining their own empires, their own power, and if that was why they had military priorities higher than bombing the rail lines leading to Auschwitz. Six million Jews were killed in the death camps (allowed to be killed?). Only 60,000 were saved by the war—1 percent.

A gunner on another crew, a reader of history with whom I had become friends, said to me one day: "You know this is an imperialist war. The fascists are evil. But our side is not much better." I could not accept his statement at the time, but it stuck with me.

War, I decided, creates, insidiously, a common morality for all sides. It poisons everyone who is engaged in it, however different they are in many ways, turns them into killers and torturers, as we are seeing now. It pretends to be concerned with toppling tyrants, and may in fact do so, but the people it kills are the victims of the tyrants. It appears to cleanse the world of evil, but that does not last, because its very nature spawns more evil. Wars, like violence in general, I concluded, is a drug. It gives a quick high, the thrill of victory, but that wears off and then comes despair.

I acknowledge the possibility of humanitarian intervention to prevent atrocities, as in Rwanda. But war, defined as the indiscriminate killing of large numbers of people, must be resisted.

Whatever can be said about World War II, understanding its complexity, the situations that followed—Korea, Vietnam—were so far from the kind of threat that Germany and Japan had posed to the world that those wars could be justified only by drawing on the glow of "the good war." A hysteria about communism led to McCarthyism at home and military interventions in Asia and Latin America—overt and covert—justified by a "Soviet threat" that was exaggerated just enough to mobilize the people for war. Vietnam, however, proved to be a sobering experience, in which the American public, over a period of several years, began to see through the lies that had been told to justify all that bloodshed. The United States was forced to withdraw from Vietnam, and the world didn't come to an end. One half of one tiny country in Southeast Asia was now joined to its communist other half, and 58,000 American lives and millions of Vietnamese lives had been expended to prevent that. A majority of Americans had come to oppose that war, which had provoked the largest anti-war movement in the nation's history.

The war in Vietnam ended with a public fed up with war. I believe that the American people, once the fog of propaganda had dissipated, had come back to a more natural state. Public opinion polls showed that people in the United States were opposed to send troops anywhere in the world, for any reason.

The Establishment was alarmed. The government set out deliberately to overcome what it called "the Vietnam syndrome." Opposition to military interventions abroad was a sickness, to be cured. And so they would wean the American public away from its unhealthy attitude, by tighter control of information, by avoiding a draft, and by engaging in short, swift wars over weak opponents (Grenada, Panama, Iraq), which didn't give the public time to develop an anti-war movement. I would argue that the end of the Vietnam War enabled the people of the United States to shake the "war syndrome," a disease not natural to the human body. But they could be infected once again, and September 11 gave the government that opportunity. Terrorism became the justification for war, but war is itself terrorism, breeding rage and hate, as we are seeing now.

The war in Iraq has revealed the hypocrisy of the "war on terrorism." And the government of the United States, indeed governments everywhere, are becoming exposed as untrustworthy: that is, not to be entrusted with the safety of human beings, or the safety of the planet, or the guarding of its air, its water, its natural wealth, or the curing of poverty and disease, or coping with the alarming growth of natural disasters that plague so many of the six billion people on Earth.

I don't believe that our government will be able to do once more what it did after Vietnam—prepare the population for still another plunge into violence and dishonor. It seems to me that when the war in Iraq ends, and the war syndrome heals, that there will be a great opportunity to make that healing permanent. My hope is that the memory of death and disgrace will be so intense that the people of the United States will be able to listen to a message that the rest of the world, sobered by wars without end, can also understand: that war itself is the enemy of the human race.

Governments will resist this message. But their power is dependent on the obedience of the citizenry. When that is withdrawn, governments are helpless. We have seen this again and again in history.

The abolition of war has become not only desirable but absolutely necessary if the planet is to be saved. It is an idea whose time has come.

25.

WHY WAR FAILS
November 2006

I suggest there is something important to be learned from the recent experience of the United States and Israel in the Middle East: that massive military attacks are not only morally reprehensible but useless in achieving the stated aims of those who carry them out.

In the three years of the Iraq War, which began with shock-and-awe bombardment and goes on with day-to-day violence and chaos, the United States has failed utterly in its claimed objective of bringing democracy and stability to Iraq. American soldiers and civilians, fearful of going into the neighborhoods of Baghdad, are huddled inside the Green Zone, where the largest embassy in the world is being built, covering 104 acres and closed off from the world outside its walls.

I remember John Hersey's novel *The War Lover*, in which a macho American pilot, who loves to drop bombs on people, and also to boast about his sexual conquests, turns out to be impotent. George Bush, strutting in his flight jacket on an aircraft carrier, and announcing victory in Iraq, has turned out to be an embodiment of the Hersey character, his words equally boastful, his military machine equally impotent.

The Israeli invasion and bombing of Lebanon has not brought security to Israel. Indeed, it has increased the number of its enemies, whether in Hezbollah or Hamas, or among Arabs who belong to neither of those groups.

That failure of massive force goes so deep into history that Israeli leaders must have been extraordinarily obtuse, or blindly fanatic, to miss it. The memory is not lost to Professor Ze'ev Maoz at Tel Aviv University, writing recently in the Israeli newspaper *Ha'aretz* about a previous Israeli invasion of Lebanon: "Approximately 14,000 civilians were killed between June and September of 1982, according to a conservative estimate." The result, aside from the physical and human devastation, was the rise of Hezbollah, whose rockets provoked another desperate exercise of massive force.

The history of wars fought since the end of World War II reveals the futility of large-scale violence. The United States and the Soviet Union, despite their enormous firepower, were unable to defeat resistance movements in small, weak nations. Even though the United States dropped more bombs in the Vietnam War than in all of World War II, it was still forced to withdraw. The Soviet Union, trying for a decade to conquer Afghanistan, in a war that caused a million deaths, became bogged down and also finally withdrew.

Even the supposed triumphs of great military powers turn out to be elusive. After attacking and invading Afghanistan, President Bush boasted that the Taliban were defeated. But five years later, Afghanistan is rife with violence, and the Taliban are active in much of the country. Last May, there were riots in Kabul, after a runaway American military truck killed five Afghans. When

U.S. soldiers fired into the crowd, four more people were killed.

After the brief, apparently victorious war against Iraq in 1991, George Bush Sr. declared (in a moment of rare eloquence): "The specter of Vietnam has been buried forever in the desert sands of the Arabian peninsula." Those sands are bloody once more.

The same George Bush presided over the military attack on Panama in 1989, which killed thousands and destroyed entire neighborhoods, justified by the "war on drugs." Another victory, but in a few years, the drug trade in Panama was thriving as before.

The nations of Eastern Europe, despite Soviet occupation, developed resistance movements that eventually compelled the Soviet military to leave. The United States, which had its way in Latin America for a hundred years, has been unable, despite a long history of military interventions, to control events in Cuba, or Venezuela, or Brazil, or Bolivia.

Overwhelming Israeli military power, while occupying the West Bank and Gaza, has not been able to stop the resistance movement of Palestinians. Israel has not made itself more secure by its continued use of massive force. The United States, despite two successive wars, in Iraq and Afghanistan, is not more secure.

More important than the futility of armed force is the fact that war in our time always results in the indiscriminate killing of large numbers of people. To put it more bluntly, war is terrorism. That is why a "war on terrorism" is a contradiction in terms. The repeated excuse for war, and its toll on civilians—and this has been uttered by Pentagon spokespersons as well as by Israeli officials—is that terrorists hide among civilians. Therefore the killing of innocent people (in Iraq, in Lebanon) is "accidental" whereas the deaths caused by terrorists (9/11, Hezbollah rockets) are deliberate.

This is a false distinction. If a bomb is deliberately dropped on a house or a vehicle on the ground that a "suspected terrorist" is inside (note the frequent use of the word "suspected" as evidence of the uncertainty surrounding targets), it is argued that the resulting deaths of women and children is not intended, therefore "accidental." The deaths of innocent people in bombing may not be intentional. Neither are they accidental. The proper description is "inevitable."

So if an action will inevitably kill innocent people, it is as immoral as a "deliberate" attack on civilians. And when you consider that the number of people dying inevitably in "accidental" events has been far greater than all the deaths of innocent people deliberately caused by terrorists, one must reconsider the morality of war, any war in our time.

It is a supreme irony that the "war on terrorism" has brought a higher death toll among innocent civilians than the hijackings of 9/11, which killed up to 3,000 people. The United States reacted to 9/11 by invading and bombing Afghanistan. In that operation, at least 3,000 civilians were killed, and hundreds of thousands were forced to flee their homes and villages, terrorized by what was supposed to be a war on terror. Bush's Iraq War, which he keeps linking to the "war on terror," has killed between 40,000 and 140,000 civilians.

More than a million civilians in Vietnam were killed by U.S. bombs, presumably by "accident." Add up all the terrorist attacks throughout the world in the twentieth century and they do not equal that awful toll.

If reacting to terrorist attacks by war is inevitably immoral, then we must look for ways other than war to end terrorism.

And if military retaliation for terrorism is not only immoral but futile, then political leaders, however cold-blooded their calculations, must reconsider their policies. When such practical considerations are joined to a rising popular revulsion against war, perhaps the long era of mass murder may be brought to an end.

26.

IMPEACHMENT BY THE PEOPLE
February 2007

Courage is in short supply in Washington, D.C. The realities of the Iraq War cry out for the overthrow of a government that is criminally responsible for death, mutilation, torture, humiliation, chaos. But all we hear in the nation's capital, which is the source of those catastrophes, is a whimper from the Democratic Party, muttering and nattering about "unity" and "bipartisanship," in a situation that calls for bold action to immediately reverse the present course.

These are the Democrats who were brought to power in November by an electorate fed up with the war, furious at the Bush administration, and counting on the new majority in Congress to represent the voters. But if sanity is to be restored in our national policies, it can only come about by a great popular upheaval, pushing both Republicans and Democrats into compliance with the national will.

The Declaration of Independence, revered as a document but ignored as a guide to action, needs to be read from pulpits and podiums, on street corners and community radio stations throughout the nation. Its words, forgotten for over two centuries, need to become a call to action for the first time since it was read aloud to crowds in the early excited days of the American Revolution: "Whenever any form of government becomes destructive of these ends, it is the right of the people to alter or abolish it and institute new government."

The "ends" referred to in the Declaration are the equal right of all to "life, liberty, and the pursuit of happiness." True, no government in the history of the nation has been faithful to those ends. Favors for the rich, neglect of the poor, massive violence in the interest of continental and world expansion—that is the persistent record of our government.

Still, there seems to be a special viciousness that accompanies the current assault on human rights, in this country and in the world. We have had repressive governments before, but none has legislated the end of habeas corpus, nor openly supported torture, nor declared the possibility of war without end. No government has so casually ignored the will of the people, affirmed the right of the president to ignore the Constitution, even to set aside laws passed by Congress.

The time is right, then, for a national campaign calling for the impeachment of President Bush and Vice President Cheney. Representative John Conyers, who held extensive hearings and introduced an impeachment resolution when the Republicans controlled Congress, is now head of the House Judiciary Committee and in a position to fight for such a resolution. He has apparently been silenced by his Democratic colleagues who throw out as nuggets of wisdom the usual political palaver about "realism" (while ignoring the realities staring them in the face) and politics being "the art of the possible" (while setting limits on what is possible).

I know I'm not the first to talk about impeachment. Indeed, judging by the public opinion polls, there are millions of Americans, indeed a majority of those polled, who declare themselves in favor if it is shown that the president lied us into war (a fact that is not debatable). There are at least a half-dozen books out on impeachment, and it's been argued for eloquently by some of our finest journalists, John Nichols and Lewis Lapham among them. Indeed, an actual "indictment" has been drawn up by a former federal prosecutor, Elizabeth de la Vega, in a new book called *United States v. George W. Bush et al.*, making a case, in devastating detail, to a fictional grand jury.

There is a logical next step in this development of an impeachment movement: the convening of "people's impeachment hearings" all over the country. This is especially important given the timidity of the Democratic Party. Such hearings would bypass Congress, which is not representing the will of the people, and would constitute an inspiring example of grassroots democracy.

These hearings would be the contemporary equivalents of the unofficial gatherings that marked the resistance to the British Crown in the years leading up to the American Revolution. The story of the American Revolution is usually built around Lexington and Concord, around the battles and the Founding Fathers. What is forgotten is that the American colonists, unable to count on redress of their grievances from the official bodies of government, took matters into their own hands, even before the first battles of the Revolutionary War.

In 1772, town meetings in Massachusetts began setting up Committees of Correspondence, and the following year, such a committee was set up in Virginia. The first Continental Congress, beginning to meet in 1774, was a recognition that an extralegal body was necessary to represent the interests of the people. In 1774 and 1775, all through the colonies, parallel institutions were set up outside the official governmental bodies.

Throughout the nation's history, the failure of government to deliver justice has led to the establishment of grassroots organizations, often ad hoc, dissolving after their purpose was fulfilled. For instance, after passage of the Fugitive Slave Act, knowing that the national government could not be counted on to repeal the act, black and white anti-slavery groups organized to nullify the law by acts of civil disobedience. They held meetings, made plans, and set about rescuing escaped slaves who were in danger of being returned to their masters.

In the desperate economic conditions of 1933 and 1934, before the Roosevelt administration was doing anything to help people in distress, local groups were formed all over the country to demand government action. Unemployed councils came into being, tenants' groups fought evictions, and hundreds of thousands of people in the country formed self-help organizations to exchange goods and services and enable people to survive.

More recently, we recall the peace groups of the 1980s, which sprang up in hundreds of communities all over the country, and provoked city councils and state legislatures to pass resolutions in favor of a freeze on nuclear weapons. And local organizations have succeeded in getting more than 400 city councils to take a stand against the Patriot Act.

Impeachment hearings all over the country could excite and energize the peace movement. They would make headlines, and could push reluctant members of Congress in both parties to do what the Constitution provides for and what the present circumstances demand: the impeachment and removal from office of George Bush and Dick Cheney. Simply raising the issue in hundreds of communities and Congressional districts would have a healthy effect, and would be a sign that democracy, despite all attempts to destroy it in this era of war, is still alive.

27.
ARE WE POLITICIANS OR CITIZENS?
May 2007

As I write this, Congress is debating timetables for withdrawal from Iraq. In response to the Bush administration's "surge" of troops, and the Republicans' refusal to limit our occupation, the Democrats are behaving with their customary timidity, proposing withdrawal, but only after a year, or eighteen months. And it seems they expect the anti-war movement to support them.

That was suggested in a recent message from MoveOn, which polled its members on the Democratic proposal, saying that progressives in Congress, "like many of us, don't think the bill goes far enough, but see it as the first concrete step to ending the war."

Ironically, and shockingly, the same bill appropriates $124 billion more in funds to carry on the war. It's as if, before the Civil War, abolitionists agreed to postpone the emancipation of the slaves for a year, or two years, or five years, and coupled this with an appropriation of funds to enforce the Fugitive Slave Act.

When a social movement adopts the compromises of legislators, it has forgotten its role, which is to push and challenge the politicians, not to fall in meekly behind them.

We who protest the war are not politicians. We are citizens. Whatever politicians may do, let them first feel the full force of citizens who speak for what is right, not for what is winnable, in a shamefully timorous Congress.

Timetables for withdrawal are not only morally reprehensible in the case of a brutal occupation (would you give a thug who invaded your house, smashed everything in sight, and terrorized your children a timetable for withdrawal?) but logically nonsensical. If our troops are preventing civil war, helping people, controlling violence, then why withdraw at all? If they are, in fact, doing the opposite—provoking civil war, hurting people, perpetuating violence—they should withdraw as quickly as ships and planes can carry them home.

It is four years since the United States invaded Iraq with a ferocious bombardment, with "shock and awe." That is enough time to decide if the presence of our troops is making the lives of the Iraqis better or worse. The evidence is overwhelming. Since the invasion, hundreds of thousands of Iraqis have died, and, according to the U.N. High Commissioner for Refugees, about two million Iraqis have left the country, and an almost equal number are internal refugees, forced out of their homes, seeking shelter elsewhere in the country.

Yes, Saddam Hussein was a brutal tyrant. But his capture and death have not made the lives of Iraqis better, as the U.S. occupation has created chaos: no clean water, rising rates of hunger, 50 percent unemployment, shortages of food, electricity, and fuel, a rise in child malnutrition and infant deaths.

Has the U.S. presence diminished violence? On the

contrary, by January 2007 the number of insurgent attacks had increased dramatically to 180 a day.

The response of the Bush administration to four years of failure is to send more troops. To add more troops matches the definition of fanaticism: If you find you're going in the wrong direction, redouble your speed. It reminds me of the physician in Europe in the early nineteenth century who decided that bloodletting would cure pneumonia. When that didn't work, he concluded that not enough blood had been let.

The Congressional Democrats' proposal is to give more funds to the war, and to set a timetable that will enable the bloodletting go on for another year or more. It is necessary, they say, to compromise, and some anti-war people have been willing to go along.

However, it is one thing to compromise when you are immediately given part of what you are demanding, if that can then be a springboard for getting more in the future. That is the situation described in the recent movie *The Wind That Shakes the Barley*, in which the Irish rebels against British rule are given a compromise solution—to have part of Ireland free, as the Irish Free State. In the movie, Irish brother fights against brother over whether to accept this compromise. But at least the acceptance of that compromise, however short of justice, created the Irish Free State.

The withdrawal timetable proposed by the Democrats gets nothing tangible, only a promise, and leaves the fulfillment of that promise in the hands of the Bush administration.

There have been similar dilemmas for the labor

movement. Indeed, it is a common occurrence that unions, fighting for a new contract, must decide if they will accept an offer that gives them only part of what they have demanded.

It's always a difficult decision, but in almost all cases, whether the compromise can be considered a victory or a defeat, the workers have been given something palpable, improving their condition to some degree. If they were offered only a promise of something in the future, while continuing an unbearable situation in the present, it would not be considered a compromise, but a sellout.

A union leader who said, "Take this, it's the best we can get" (which is what the MoveOn people are saying about the Democrats' resolution) would be hooted off the platform.

I am reminded of the situation at the 1964 Democratic National Convention in Atlantic City, when the black delegation from Mississippi asked to be seated so as to give representation to the 40 percent black population of that state. They were offered a "compromise"— two nonvoting seats. "This is the best we can get," some black leaders said. The Mississippians, led by Fannie Lou Hamer and Bob Moses, turned it down, and thus held on to their fighting spirit, which later brought them what they had asked for.

That mantra—"the best we can get"—is a recipe for corruption.

It is not easy, in the corrupting atmosphere of Washington, D.C., to hold on firmly to the truth, to resist the temptation of capitulation that presents itself as compromise. A few manage to do so. I think of Barbara Lee, the one person in the House of Representatives who, in the hysterical atmosphere of the days following 9/11, voted against the resolution authorizing Bush to invade Afghanistan. Today, she is one of the few who refuse to fund the Iraq War, insist on a prompt end to the war, reject the dishonesty of a false compromise. Except for the rare few, like Barbara Lee, Maxine Waters, Lynn Woolsey, Dennis Kucinich, and John Lewis, our representatives are politicians, and will surrender their integrity, claiming to be "realistic."

We are not politicians, but citizens.

We have no office to hold on to, only our consciences, which insist on telling the truth.

That, history suggests, is the most realistic thing a citizen can do.

28

KURT VONNEGUT REMEMBERED
June 2007

Kurt Vonnegut, who died recently at eighty-four, liked to quote Eugene Debs, when Debs addressed the judge who sentenced him to ten years in prison for protesting U.S. entrance into the First World War: "Your honor, years ago I recognized my kinship with all living beings and I made up my mind that I was not one bit better than the meanest on Earth. I said then, and I say now, that while there is a lower class, I am in it; while there is a criminal element, I am of it; while there is a soul in prison, I am not free."

Kurt Vonnegut and I became friends about ten years ago, when he phoned me, out of the blue. He had a rich telephone voice: "Hello, this is Kurt Vonnegut. That's a damn good piece you wrote on Machiavelli and U.S. foreign policy." After that, we would talk on the phone from time to time. We had things in common: the Second World War, bombing, books, the future of the world. He was gloomy about the ongoing destruction of the planet, yet had faith in the capacity of ordinary human beings to resist stupidity.

When he phoned, there was always something specific on his mind, an event in the news, or, one time, the death of his friend Joseph Heller, whom Kurt affectionately called "a holy clown." Heller's novel *Catch-22* has the wild humor and dead seriousness of Vonnegut's *Slaughterhouse-Five*, both bitter-comic commentaries on war, uninhibited by all the romanticization of "the good war."

Slaughterhouse-Five came out of Vonnegut's experience as a prisoner of war in Dresden, trapped—fortunately—in a meat locker underground as U.S. and British planes turned the city into an inferno, causing the deaths of perhaps 100,000 people.

In the book, his alter ego is an innocent young American named Billy Pilgrim, who emerges from the meat locker the day after the bombing and sees a sky black with smoke. "The sun was an angry little pinhead. Dresden was like the moon now, nothing but minerals. The stones were hot. Everybody else in the neighborhood was dead. So it goes."

Kurt Vonnegut had a profound hatred of war. Hiroshima and Nagasaki were never far from his mind. He could not abide the slaughter in Vietnam, or the hypocrisy of the United States government holding on to thousands of nuclear weapons while creating hysteria about any other nation that might develop one.

When the newspapers were full of alarms about Iran possibly developing a nuclear bomb, Kurt sent me a copy of a very short letter he wrote to the *New York Times*: "I know of only one nation that has dropped nuclear bombs on innocent people."

The *Times* did not print the letter.

He spoke at rallies against the Vietnam War, against the first Gulf War in 1991, and was agonized by the present war in Iraq. We had lunch one day in Manhattan a few blocks from the midtown brownstone where he lived with his wife, the photographer Jill Krementz. We talked about the need, beyond this war, to abolish all wars, whatever the reason. Sometime after that my wife, Roslyn, with whom he had become telephone friends, received from him a large framed print of a 1924 Kathe Kollwitz painting showing a young person with a hand raised to the sky, crying out "Nie wieder Krieg" ("No More War").

Roslyn wrote to a friend after learning of Kurt's death: "The loss of Kurt Vonnegut is profound in our lives. We were lucky enough to meet him when in early 2003 he read in New York at the 92nd St. Y the words of Eugene Debs and Mark Twain. He was terrific. . . . He has been a wonderful correspondent to both of us. (He didn't do e-mail but loved to talk on the telephone and to write letters.) He would send graphics that he would dash off with his pithy, outrageous comments, and they hang in my study."

Sometime in the 1960s, Kurt Vonnegut's fourth novel was published and became a huge success. This was *Cat's Cradle*, which by 1980 had gone through fifty-one printings. Its flights of fancy, in which were buried delicious nuggets of wisdom, caught the imagination of a whole generation. He did not hesitate to create a new vocabulary.

The word *granfaloon* is now known to millions of his readers. It means an artificial assemblage of people, "a seeming team that was meaningless in terms of the ways God gets things done" He gives as examples: "the Communist Party, the Daughters of the American Revolution, the General Electric Company, the International Order of Odd Fellows—and any nation, anytime, anywhere."

A *karass*, on the other hand, is a group of people who may not know one another but who are connected in a very human way, because "a *karass* ignores national, institutional, occupational, familial, and class boundaries."

Kurt was class-conscious to the bone. Hence his admiration for Debs, the Socialist. He was an agnostic for whom socialism was godliness and Christ was a radical organizer, and the Bible, whatever dubious passages it might have, also saw all God's creatures as equal. In his book *Jailbird*, he tells of Powers Hapgood (a real person), who graduated from Harvard but becomes a labor organizer and leads a strike against an RCA plant in New Jersey. Hapgood is jailed, then brought before a judge who asks him: "Mr. Hapgood, why would a man from such a distinguished family and with such a fine education choose to live as you do?" Hapgood replies: "Why? Because of the Sermon on the Mount, sir."

In the same book, Kurt Vonnegut quotes Nicola Sacco's last letter to his thirteen-year-old son, Dante, just days before Sacco's execution: "Help the weak ones that cry for me, help the persecuted and the victim, because they are your better friends; they are the comrades that fight and fall as your father and Bartolo [Vanzetti] fought and fell yesterday for the conquest of the joy of freedom for all the poor workers. In this struggle of life you will find more love and you will be loved."

In *Jailbird*, Vonnegut is amused at the pretensions of capitalism, the assumption that cleverness in business will get you into heaven. He has a story within his story, written by a favorite character of his, Kilgore Trout, called

"Asleep at the Switch." It's about a huge reception center outside the Pearly Gates—filled with computers and staffed by people who have been certified public accountants or investment counselors or business managers back on Earth. "And you couldn't get into heaven unless you had handled well the business opportunities which God had offered you. And to those who had failed to make the most of these opportunities, the experts would deny admittance, saying: 'And there you were, asleep at the switch again.' Albert Einstein, it turns out, has missed all sorts of opportunities to invest in stocks and make millions, and he cannot get into Heaven. He is told, 'There you were, asleep at the switch again.' "

Kurt Vonnegut's novels became more personal, more pointedly political. His last one, *Timequake*, is part novel, part memoir. He asks: "Should the nation's wealth be redistributed? It has been and continues to be redistributed to a few people in a manner strikingly unhelpful. . . . Faithless custodians of capital [are] making themselves multimillionaires and multibillionaires, while playing beanbag with money better spent on creating meaningful jobs, and training people to fill them, and raising our young and retiring our old in surroundings of respect and safety. For Christ's sake, let's help more of our frightened people get through this thing, whatever it is." Kurt expressed his agnosticism through wry humor, laced with bitterness.

In *Jailbird*, he has one of his characters, a concentration camp survivor named Ruth, reply to a question: Had she ever sought the consolations of religion in the concentration camp? "No," she said. "I knew God would never come near such a place. So did the Nazis. . . . They understood God better than anyone." One Christmas Eve, Ruth offers a toast: "Here's to God Almighty, the laziest man in town."

But he could get past the bitterness, too. In *Timequake*, he tells of a woman who wrote to him, saying she was pregnant and wondered if it was a mistake to bring a baby into a world so bad. "I replied that what made being alive almost worthwhile for me was the saints I met, people behaving unselfishly and capably. They turned up in the most unexpected places. Perhaps you, dear reader, are or can become a saint for her sweet child to meet."

Kurt Vonnegut was often asked why he bothered writing. He answered this way: "Many people need desperately to receive this message: 'I feel and think much as you do, care about many of the things you care about, although most people don't care about them. You are not alone.'" Millions and millions of people, all over the world, reading him, do not feel alone. What could be a more important achievement?

29.
ELECTION MADNESS
March 2008

There's a man in Florida who has been writing to me for years (ten pages, handwritten) though I've never met him. He tells me the kinds of jobs he has held—security guard, repairman, etc. He has worked all kinds of shifts, night and day, to barely keep his family going. His letters to me have always been angry, railing against our capitalist system for its failure to assure "life, liberty, the pursuit of happiness" for working people.

Just today, a letter came. To my relief it was not handwritten because he is now using e-mail:

"Well, I'm writing to you today because there is a wretched situation in this country that I cannot abide and must say something about. I am so enraged about this mortgage crisis. That the majority of Americans must live their lives in perpetual debt, and so many are sinking beneath the load, has me so steamed. Damn, that makes me so mad, I can't tell you. . . . I did a security guard job today that involved watching over a house that had been foreclosed on and was up for auction. They held an open house, and I was there to watch over the place during this event. There were three of the guards doing the same thing in three other homes in this same community. I was sitting there during the quiet moments and wondering about who those people were who had been evicted and where they were now."

On the same day I received this letter, there was a front-page story in the *Boston Globe*, with the headline "Thousands in Mass. Foreclosed on in '07."

The subhead was "7,563 homes were seized, nearly 3 times the '06 rate."

A few nights before, CBS television reported that 750,000 people with disabilities have been waiting for years for their Social Security benefits because the system is underfunded and there are not enough personnel to handle all the requests, even desperate ones.

Stories like these may be reported in the media, but they are gone in a flash. What's not gone, what occupies the press day after day, impossible to ignore, is the election frenzy.

This seizes the country every four years because we have all been brought up to believe that voting is crucial in determining our destiny, that the most important act a citizen can engage in is to go to the polls and choose one of the two mediocrities who have already been chosen for us. It is a multiple choice test so narrow, so specious, that no self-respecting teacher would give it to students.

And sad to say, the presidential contest has mesmerized liberals and radicals alike. We are all vulnerable.

Is it possible to get together with friends these days and avoid the subject of the presidential elections?

The very people who should know better, having criticized the hold of the media on the national mind, find themselves transfixed by the press, glued to the television set, as the candidates preen and smile and bring forth a shower of clichés with a solemnity appropriate for epic poetry.

Even in the so-called left periodicals, we must admit there is an exorbitant amount of attention given to minutely examining the major candidates. An occasional bone is thrown to the minor candidates, though everyone knows our marvelous democratic political system won't allow them in.

No, I'm not taking some ultra-left position that elections are totally insignificant, and that we should refuse to vote to preserve our moral purity. Yes, there are candidates who are somewhat better than others, and at certain times of national crisis (the 1930s, for instance, or right now) where even a slight difference between the two parties may be a matter of life and death.

I'm talking about a sense of proportion that gets lost in the election madness. Would I support one candidate against another? Yes, for two minutes—the amount of time it takes to pull the lever down in the voting booth.

But before and after those two minutes, our time, our energy, should be spent in educating, agitating, organizing our fellow citizens in the workplace, in the neighborhood, in the schools. Our objective should be to build, painstakingly, patiently but energetically, a movement that, when it reaches a certain critical mass, would shake whoever is in the White House, in Congress, into changing national policy on matters of war and social justice.

Let's remember that even when there is a "better" candidate (yes, better Roosevelt than Hoover, better anyone than George Bush), that difference will not mean anything unless the power of the people asserts itself in ways that the occupant of the White House will find it dangerous to ignore.

The unprecedented policies of the New Deal—Social Security, unemployment insurance, job creation, minimum wage, subsidized housing—were not simply the result of FDR's progressivism. The Roosevelt administration, coming into office, faced a nation in turmoil. The last year of the Hoover administration had experienced the rebellion of the Bonus Army—thousands of veterans of the First World War descending on Washington to demand help from Congress as their families were going hungry. There were disturbances of the unemployed in Detroit, Chicago, Boston, New York, Seattle. In 1934, early in the Roosevelt presidency, strikes broke out all over the country, including a general strike in Minneapolis, a general strike in San Francisco, hundreds of thousands on strike in the textile mills of the South. Unemployed councils formed all over the country. Desperate people were taking action on their own, defying the police to put back the furniture of evicted tenants, and creating self-help organizations with hundreds of thousands of members.

Without a national crisis—economic destitution and rebellion—it is not likely the Roosevelt administration would have instituted the bold reforms that it did.

Today, we can be sure that the Democratic Party, unless it faces a popular upsurge, will not move off center. The two leading presidential candidates have made it clear that if elected, they will not bring an immediate end to the Iraq War, or institute a system of free health care for all. They offer no radical change from the status quo.

They do not propose what the present desperation

of people cries out for: a government guarantee of jobs to everyone who needs one, a minimum income for every household, housing relief to everyone who faces eviction or foreclosure.

They do not suggest the deep cuts in the military budget or the radical changes in the tax system that would free billions, even trillions, for social programs to transform the way we live.

None of this should surprise us. The Democratic Party has broken with its historic conservatism, its pandering to the rich, its predilection for war, only when it has encountered rebellion from below, as in the 1930s and the 1960s. We should not expect that a victory at the ballot box in November will even begin to budge the nation from its twin fundamental illnesses: capitalist greed and militarism.

So we need to free ourselves from the election madness engulfing the entire society, including the left. Yes, two minutes. Before that, and after that, we should be taking direct action against the obstacles to life, liberty, and the pursuit of happiness.

For instance, the mortgage foreclosures that are driving millions from their homes—they should remind us of a similar situation after the Revolutionary War, when small farmers, many of them war veterans (like so many of our homeless today), could not afford to pay their taxes and were threatened with the loss of the land, their homes. They gathered by the thousands around courthouses and refused to allow the auctions to take place.

The evictions today of people who cannot pay their rents should remind us of what people did in the 1930s when they organized and put the belongings of the evicted families back in their apartments, in defiance of the authorities.

Historically, government, whether in the hands of Republicans or Democrats, conservatives or liberals, has failed its responsibilities, until forced to by direct action: sit-ins and Freedom Rides for the rights of black people, strikes and boycotts for the rights of workers, mutinies and desertions of soldiers in order to stop a war.

Voting is easy and marginally useful, but it is a poor substitute for democracy, which requires direct action by concerned citizens.

30.
THE OBAMA DIFFERENCE
October 2008

It seems that Barack Obama and John McCain are arguing over which war to fight. McCain says: Keep the troops in Iraq until we "win." Obama says: Withdraw some (not all) troops from Iraq and send them to fight and "win" in Afghanistan.

As someone who has fought in a war (World War II) and since then has protested against war, I must ask: Have our political leaders gone mad? Have they learned nothing from recent history? Have they not learned that no one "wins" in a war, but that hundreds of thousands of human beings die, most of them civilians, many of them children?

Did we "win" by going to war in Korea? The result was a stalemate, leaving things as they were before: a dictatorship in South Korea, a dictatorship in North Korea—but more than two million people, mostly civilians, were dead, and we dropped napalm on children, and 50,000 American soldiers lost their lives.

Did we "win" in Vietnam? The answer is obvious. We were forced to withdraw, but only after two million Vietnamese died, again mostly civilians, again leaving children burned or armless or legless, and 58,000 American soldiers dead.

Did we "win" in the first Gulf War? Not really. Yes, we pushed Saddam Hussein out of Kuwait with only a few hundred U.S. casualties, but we killed tens of thousands of Iraqis in the process. And the consequences were deadly for us: Saddam still in power, leading us to enforce economic sanctions that led to the deaths (according to U.N. officials) of hundreds of thousands of Iraqis, and setting the stage for another war.

In Afghanistan, we declared "victory" over the Taliban but the Taliban is back, with the attacks increasing, and our casualties in Afghanistan currently exceeding those in Iraq. What makes Obama think that sending more troops to Afghanistan will produce "victory"? And if it did, in an immediate military sense, how long would that last, and at what cost to human life on both sides?

The resurgence of fighting in Afghanistan is a good moment to reflect on the beginning of our involvement there. Let me offer some sobering thoughts to those who say, as many do: Attacking Iraq was wrong, but attacking Afghanistan was right.

Go back to 9/11. Hijackers direct jet planes into the World Trade Center and the Pentagon, killing close to 3,000 people. A terrorist act, inexcusable by any moral code. The nation is aroused. President Bush orders the invasion and bombing of Afghanistan, and the American public is swept into approval by a wave of fear and anger. Bush announces a "war on terror."

We are all (except for terrorists) against terror. So a war on terror sounds right. But there was a problem, which most Americans did not consider in the heat of the moment: We had no idea how to make war against terror; nor did Bush, despite his bravado.

Yes, Al Qaeda—a relatively small but ruthless group of fanatics—was apparently responsible. And there was evidence that its leaders, Osama Bin Laden and others, were based in Afghanistan. But we did not know exactly where. So we invaded and bombed the whole country. That made many people feel righteous: "We had to do something," you heard people say.

Yes, we had to do something. But not thoughtlessly, not recklessly. Would we approve a police chief, who, knowing there was a vicious criminal somewhere in a neighborhood, ordered that the neighborhood be bombed? There was soon a civilian death toll in Afghanistan of over 3,000—exceeding the number of deaths on 9/11. Numerous Afghans were driven from their homes, turned into wandering refugees.

A *Boston Globe* reporter, two months after the invasion of Afghanistan, described a ten-year-old boy in a hospital bed: "He lost his eyes and hands to the bomb that hit his house after Sunday dinner." The doctor attending him said, "The United States must be thinking he is Osama. If he is not Osama, then why would they do this?"

We should be asking the presidential candidates: Is our war in Afghanistan, which both of them approve, ending terrorism, or provoking it? And is not war itself terrorism?

One might assume from the above that I see no difference between McCain and Obama, that I see them as equivalent. Not so. There is a difference, not a significant enough difference for me to have confidence in Obama as president, but just enough for me to vote for Obama and to hope he defeats McCain. Whoever is president, the crucial factor for change will be how much agitation there is in the country on behalf of change. I am guessing that Obama may be more sensitive than McCain to such turmoil, since it will come from his supporters, from the enthusiasts who will register their disillusionment by taking to the streets. Franklin D. Roosevelt was not a radical, but he was more sensitive to the economic crisis in the country and more susceptible to pressure from the Left than was Herbert Hoover.

Even for the "purest" of radicals, there must be recognition of differences that may mean life or death for thousands. In France at the time of the Algerian War, the election of DeGaulle—hardly an anti-imperialist but more aware of the inevitable decline of empires—was significant in ending that long and brutal occupation.

I have no doubt that by far the wisest, most reliable, with the most integrity, of all recent presidential candidates is Ralph Nader. But I think it is a waste of his political strength, a puny act, to expend it in the electoral arena, where the result can show only weakness. His power, his intelligence, lies in the mobilization of people outside the ballot box.

So, yes, I will vote for Obama, because the corrupt political system offers me no choice, but only for the moment I pull down the lever in the voting booth.

Before and after that moment I want to use whatever energy I have to push him toward a recognition that he must defy the traditional thinkers and corporate interests surrounding him, and pay homage to the millions of Americans who want real change.

One more clarification. My lessons from history about the futility of "winning" should not be understood as meaning that what is wrong with our policy in Iraq is that we can't "win." It's not that we can't win. It's that we shouldn't win, because it's not our country.

31.
THE NOBEL'S FEEBLE GESTURE
January 2010

I don't like to annoy my readers. Who else can I count on? There are not so many that I can afford to antagonize some of them. But sometimes it happens. In this case, it was all because I received a phone call from the *Guardian* of London informing me that Barack Obama had been awarded the Nobel Peace Prize, and wondering if I would write something brief in response to that news. I sat down and dashed something off. "Ah," you say, "dashed off," suggesting that I didn't think too much before I wrote it. True, but when I read afterward what I had said, I didn't want to change a word. The little piece was printed in the *Guardian* and reprinted on *Common Dreams*—thus reaching people both in Europe and in this country.

I began getting responses, from both continents. Interestingly enough, the messages I got from abroad agreed vigorously with me.

The responses in this country were mixed, and enough of them showed annoyance, even anger, at what I said, for me to think: I must respond. At moments like that, I turn to Matt Rothschild and the *Progressive* to give me space. I guessed that the *New York Times* and CBS News would not be as welcoming.

So I will say here what I wrote for the *Guardian*, and then discuss the arguments made by critics of my piece. I do this not just because I think it will make an interesting exchange, but because I think that the issue of the prize raises a larger question: What is the role of a progressive—a progressive, a radical—in this two-party system?

So here is the original sin, and then my reaction to those who were as troubled by my little essay as I was by the action of the Nobel committee.

I was dismayed when I heard Obama was given the Nobel Peace Prize. A shock, really, to think that a president carrying on two wars would be given a peace prize. Until I recalled that Woodrow Wilson, Theodore Roosevelt, and Henry Kissinger had all received Nobel Peace Prizes. The Nobel committee is famous for its superficial estimates—won over by rhetoric and by empty gestures—and for ignoring blatant violations of world peace. Yes, Wilson gets credit for the League of Nations— that ineffectual body that did nothing to prevent war. But he had bombarded the Mexican coast, sent troops to occupy Haiti and the Dominican Republic, and brought the United States into the slaughterhouse of Europe in the First World War—surely among stupid and deadly wars at the top of the list.

Yes, Theodore Roosevelt brokered a peace between Japan and Russia. But he was a lover of war, who participated in the U.S. conquest of Cuba, pretending to liberate it from Spain while fastening U.S. chains on that tiny island. And as president he presided over the bloody war to subjugate the Filipinos, even congratulating a U.S. general who had just massacred 600 helpless villagers in the Philippines. The committee did not give the Nobel prize to Mark Twain, who denounced Roosevelt and criticized the war, or to William James, leader of the Anti-Imperialist League.

Oh, yes, the Committee saw fit to give a peace prize to Henry Kissinger, because he signed the final peace agreement ending the war in Vietnam, of which he had been one of the architects. Kissinger, who obsequiously went along with Nixon's expansion of the war, with the bombing of peasant villages in Vietnam, Laos, and Cambodia. Kissinger, who matches the definition of a war criminal very accurately, was given a peace prize!

People should be given a peace prize not on the basis of promises they have made (as with Obama, an eloquent maker of promises) but on the basis of actual accomplishments toward ending war, and Obama has continued deadly, inhuman military action in Iraq, Afghanistan, and Pakistan.

The Nobel peace committee should retire, and turn over its huge funds to some international peace organization which is not awed by stardom and rhetoric, and which has some understanding of history.

Now what's wrong with that? How can a progressive disagree? I always think that what I write makes such sense that hardly anyone will disagree. I'm obviously mistaken. I will paraphrase the critical comments and try to respond. Perhaps the most frequent argument is that the Nobel Committee understood that Obama's actual accomplishments didn't justify the prize, but his promises, during and after his presidential campaign, gave hope that the prize might spur him to live up to those promises. Indeed, Obama himself, in respectfully accepting the award, was a model of modesty, not claiming accomplishments, but seeing the prize as an encouragement to actions on behalf of world peace.

I can understand the impulse to make the most of the situation, but there is only a remote possibility that the prize will have the desired effect. The proponents of this theory assume that Obama's conscience will be moved by the prize, as if he is a lone actor, with the freedom to respond to that generous offering. But he is not a lone actor. He is the top man, yes, but he stands at the apex of a pyramid of power that has layer after layer of corporatists and militarists.

Nor has he tried to dismantle this pyramid. Far from it. He himself has appointed the hawkish Hillary Clinton and Joe Biden, and he has kept on Robert Gates as defense secretary, a holdover from the last two Bush administrations. None of his advisers has shown any inclination to move boldly away from war and militarism.

Yes, Obama can make eloquent speeches, but he has not been able to turn these speeches into action, because he himself is responsible for maintaining the pyramid of power.

Can a peace prize give Obama the enormous strength he would need to reverse the policies of his predecessor, and also those policies of his own which are in line with those of his predecessor? I doubt it very much.

What if the Nobel committee in 1965 or 1966 had decided to give the Peace Prize to Lyndon Johnson, on the supposition that this would encourage him to withdraw from Vietnam? Can anyone imagine that would work? That feeble gesture (and prizes are usually feeble gestures thrown into the hard world of power and profit) would hardly budge the phalanx of generals and hawkish advisers urging Johnson to escalate the war.

Some people have responded to my article by pointing to the fact that Obama has been in office less than a year, and that this is not enough time for him to overcome the enormous weight of the Bush policies. That argument might be persuasive, if we saw even the smallest move (other than words and promises) in the direction of lightening that weight. Indeed, Obama's policies have reinforced Bush's in Iraq, by continuing that war despite token troop withdrawals, while doing nothing to remove the private armies which, with profitable contracts, have been among the chief oppressors of the Iraqi people.

Obama has actually gone beyond Bush in carrying out violent actions in two places: Afghanistan, where he has sent more troops, and where our air strikes have continued to kill innocent people; and Pakistan, where, almost immediately as he took office, he sent unmanned missiles across the border, causing hundreds of civilian casualties. Those Predator missiles continue to be launched against Pakistan, and continue to kill inhabitants, under the guise of hunting down "suspected terrorists."

Obama, even in his short time in office, has had an opportunity to reduce, even by a little, the huge military budget of over $600 billion. Instead, he has increased it. To say that he has not had enough time to overcome Bush's policies makes no sense if Obama is the one who is continuing and even enhancing those policies.

I think some progressives have forgotten the history of the Democratic Party, to which people have turned again and again in desperate search for saviors, later to be disappointed. Our political history shows us that only great popular movements, carrying out bold actions that awakened the nation and threatened the Establishment, as in the thirties and the sixties, have been able to shake that pyramid of corporate and military power and at least temporarily change course.

Obama, far more likely than Bush, might respond to such a national movement, which would demand bold change. That's what it will take. Today. To award him a prize, to applaud his rhetoric, is by no means a substitute for such a movement.

32.

THREE HOLY WARS
July 2009

I want to talk about three holy wars. They aren't religious wars, but they're the three wars in American history that are sacrosanct, that you can't say anything bad about: the Revolutionary War, the Civil War, and World War II. Let's look carefully at these three idealized, three romanticized wars.

It's important to at least be willing to raise the possibility that you could criticize something that everybody has accepted as uncriticizable.

We're supposed to be thinking people. We're supposed to be able to question everything.

There are things that happen in the world that are bad, and you want to do something about them. You have a just cause. But our culture is so war prone that we immediately jump from "This is a good cause" to "This deserves a war."

You need to be very, very careful in making that jump.

You might say it was a good cause to get Spain out of Cuba in 1898. Spain was oppressing Cuba. But did that necessarily mean we needed to go to war against Spain? We have to see what it produced. We got Spain out of oppressing Cuba and got ourselves into oppressing Cuba.

You might say that stopping North Korea from invading South Korea was a good idea. The North Koreans shouldn't have done that. It wasn't good. It wasn't right. Does that mean we should have gone to war to stop it? Especially when you consider that two or three million Koreans died in that war? And what did the war accomplish? It started off with a dictatorship in South Korea and a dictatorship in North Korea. And it ended up, after two to three million dead, with a dictatorship in South Korea and a dictatorship in North Korea.

I'd be very careful about rushing from one thing to another, from just cause to just war.

The American Revolution—independence from England—was a just cause. Why should the colonists here be oppressed by England? But therefore, did we have to go to the Revolutionary War? How many people died in the Revolutionary War?

Nobody ever knows exactly how many people die in wars, but it's likely that 25,000 to 50,000 people died in this one. So let's take the lower figure—25,000 people died out of a population of three million. That would be equivalent today to two and a half million people dying to get England off our backs.

You might consider that worth it, or you might not.

Canada is independent of England, isn't it? Not a bad society. Canadians have good health care. They have a lot of things we don't have. They didn't fight a bloody revolutionary war. Why do we assume that we had to fight a bloody revolutionary war to get rid of England?

In the year before those famous shots were fired, farmers in Western Massachusetts had driven the British government out without firing a single shot. They had assembled by the thousands and thousands around court-houses and colonial offices and they had just taken over and they said goodbye to the British officials. It was a nonviolent revolution that took place. But then came Lexington and Concord, and the revolution became violent, and it was run not by the farmers but by the Founding Fathers. The farmers were rather poor; the Founding Fathers were rather rich.

Who actually gained from that victory over England? It's very important to ask about any policy, and especially about war: Who gained what? And it's very important to notice differences among the various parts of the population. That's one thing we're not accustomed to in this country because we don't think in class terms. We think, "Oh, we all have the same interests." For instance, we think that we all had the same interests in independence from England. We did not have all the same interests.

Do you think the Indians cared about independence from England? No, in fact, the Indians were unhappy that we won independence from England, because England had set a line—in the Proclamation of 1763—that said you couldn't go westward into Indian territory. They didn't do it because they loved the Indians but because they didn't want trouble. When Britain was defeated in the Revolutionary War, that line was eliminated, and now the way was open for the colonists to move westward across the continent, which they did for the next 100 years, committing massacres and making sure that they destroyed Indian civilization.

Did blacks benefit from the American Revolution? Slavery was there before. Slavery was there after.

Not only that, we wrote slavery into the Constitution. We legitimized it.

What about class divisions?

Did ordinary white farmers have the same interest in the revolution as a John Hancock or Robert Morris or Madison or Jefferson or the slaveholders or the bondholders? Not really.

It was not all the common people getting together to fight against England. The founders had a very hard time assembling an army. They took poor guys and promised them land. They browbeat people and, oh, yes, they inspired people with the Declaration of Independence. It's always important, if you want people to go to war, to give them a fine document and have good words: life, liberty, and the pursuit of happiness. Of course, when they wrote the Constitution, they were more concerned with the pursuit of property than the pursuit of happiness. You should take notice of these little things.

We were a class society from the beginning. America started off as a society of rich and poor, people with enormous grants of land and people with no land. And there were bread riots in Boston, and flour riots and rebellions all over the colonies, of poor against rich, of tenants breaking into jails to release people who were in prison for nonpayment of debt. There was class conflict. We try to pretend in this country that we're all one happy family. We're not.

Do you know that there were mutinies in the American Revolutionary Army by the privates against the officers? The officers were getting fine clothes and good food and high pay and the privates had no shoes and bad clothes and they weren't getting paid. They mutinied. Thousands of them. So many in the Pennsylvania line that George Washington got worried, so he made compromises with them. But later when there was a smaller mutiny in the New Jersey line, not with thousands but with hundreds, Washington said execute the leaders, and they were executed by fellow mutineers on the order of their officers.

The American Revolution was not a simple affair of all of us against all of them.

When considering war you need to weigh the human cost against what you gain from war. When you think about the human cost, generally it's an abstraction: 25,000 people died in the Revolutionary War; 600,000 people died in the Civil War; fifty million people died in World War II. But you have to look at that cost not as an abstraction, not as a statistic. You have to look at it as every human being who died, every human being who lost a limb, every human being who came out blind, and every human being who came out mentally damaged. You have to put all of that together when you're assessing that side of the ledger: the cost of the war. Before you ask, "Was it worth it? Was it a just war?" you've got to get that side of the ledger right. Now, the Civil War was an ugly, brutal war. The 600,000 people died is equivalent to five million today. Plus, there was amputation after amputation after amputation done in the field without anesthesia. The real human costs were enormous. Who gained?

In the Civil War, we learn about the North versus South, the Blue versus the Gray. But who in the North? Who in the South? What class divisions were there?

Poor white people were conscripted into a war that didn't have much meaning for them. They were being drafted when the rich could get out of the war by paying

$300. So there were draft riots in New York and other cities. There was class conflict in the North. There were some people in the North who got rich during the war. J. P. Morgan made a fortune. That's what wars do: They make some people very rich. And it's the poor who go to fight in the wars.

There was class conflict in the Confederacy, too. Most whites were not slaveowners. Maybe one out of six whites was a slaveowner. Poor white soldiers in the South were dying at a much higher rate than the soldiers of the North. As the mayhem went on, as the bloodshed magnified, their families back home were starving because the plantation owners were growing cotton instead of food. And so the wives and the daughters and the girlfriends and the sisters, they began to riot in Georgia and Alabama in protest against the fact that their sons and husbands were dying while the plantation owners were getting rich.

I mustn't ignore the positive side of the Civil War. Yes, emancipation. Freeing the slaves. That's no small matter. You can say maybe the 600,000 dead were worth it if you really freed four million black people and brought them into freedom. But they weren't exactly brought into freedom. They were brought into semi-slavery. They were betrayed by the politicians and the financiers of the North. They were left without resources. They were left at the mercy of the same plantation owners who owned them as slaves and now they were serfs. They couldn't move from one place to another. They were hemmed in by all sorts of restrictions, and many of them were put in jail on false charges. And vagrancy statutes were passed so that employers could pick up blacks off the street and force them to work in a kind of slave labor.

So to say that maybe it was OK that 600,000 people died because we ended slavery is not so simple.

Is it possible that slavery could have ended another way, without 600,000 people dead? That's something we don't think of. Just like we don't think of, "Could we have won independence from England without a bloody war?" Remember, there were other countries in the Western Hemisphere that ended slavery without a bloody civil war.

I volunteered to be in World War II and flew bombing missions over Europe. I did it because it was "the good war," it was the right war, it was a just war. After I got out of the war, I began to go back over things and learn about Hiroshima and Nagasaki. When Truman dropped the bomb on Hiroshima, I had just finished my missions in Europe, and was going to go to the Pacific for more missions. So when the war ended soon after Hiroshima, I thought, "Wow, that's great!" I welcomed it. Did I really know what happened when that bomb was dropped on Hiroshima? Did I have any idea what that meant to those hundreds of thousands of people—men, women, and children? No, I did not. When I began to think about it, then I began to think about the people under my bombs. I never saw them. I was flying 30,000 feet above them. I began to learn something about the reality of Dresden. And I began to learn that three months before Hiroshima and Nagasaki, we sent planes over to firebomb Tokyo, and 100,000 people were killed in one night. Later, when I visited Japan and I visited Hiroshima, I met with survivors of Hiroshima—people without legs and without arms and blind and so on—I began to see what that war meant.

Well, you say, we defeated fascism. Did we, really?

Fifty million people dead, and yes, you got rid of Hitler and the Japanese military machine and Mussolini. But did you get rid of fascism in the world? Did you get rid of militarism? Did you get rid of racism? Did you get rid of war? We've had war after war after war. What did those fifty million die for?

We've got to rethink this question of war and come to the conclusion that war cannot be accepted, no matter what. No matter what the reasons given, or the excuse: liberty, democracy; this, that. War is by definition the indiscriminate killing of huge numbers of people for ends that are uncertain. Think about means and ends, and apply it to war. The means are horrible, certainly. The ends, uncertain. That alone should make you hesitate.

People always ask me, "Yeah, but what else were we to do about this, or that? Independence from England, slavery, Hitler?"

I agree, you had to do something about all these things. But you don't have to do war.

Once a historical event has taken place—Hitler invades Czechoslovakia and Poland, for instance—it becomes very hard to imagine that you could have achieved a result some other way. When something is happening in history, it takes on a certain air of inevitability: This is the only way it could have happened. No.

We are smart in so many ways. Surely, we should be able to understand that in between war and passivity, there are a thousand possibilities.

33.

THEY RIOTED IF NECESSARY
May 2009

We are citizens, and Obama is a politician. You might not like that word. But the fact is he's a politician. He's other things, too—he's a very sensitive and intelligent and thoughtful and promising person. But he's a politician.

If you're a citizen, you have to know the difference between them and you—the difference between what they have to do and what you have to do. And there are things they *don't* have to do, if you make it clear to them they don't have to do it.

From the beginning, I liked Obama. But the first time it suddenly struck me that he was a politician was early on, when Joe Lieberman was running for the Democratic nomination for his Senate seat in 2006.

Lieberman—who, as you know, was and is a war lover—was running for the Democratic nomination, and his opponent was a man named Ned Lamont, who was the peace candidate. And Obama went to Connecticut to support Lieberman against Lamont.

It took me aback. I say that to indicate that, yes, Obama was and is a politician. So we must not be swept away into an unthinking and unquestioning acceptance of what Obama does.

Our job is not to give him a blank check or simply be cheerleaders. It was good that we were cheerleaders while he was running for office, but it's not good to be cheerleaders now. Because we want the country to go beyond where it has been in the past. We want to make a clean break from what it has been in the past.

I had a teacher at Columbia University named Richard Hofstadter, who wrote a book called *The American Political Tradition*, and in it, he examined presidents from the Founding Fathers down through Franklin Roosevelt. There were liberals and conservatives, Republicans and Democrats. And there were differences between them. But he found that the so-called liberals were not as liberal as people thought—and that the difference between the liberals and the conservatives, and between Republicans and Democrats, was not a polar difference. There was a common thread that ran through all American history, and all of the presidents—Republican, Democrat, liberal, conservative—followed this thread. The thread consisted of two elements: one, nationalism; and two, capitalism. And Obama is not yet free of that powerful double heritage.

We can see it in the policies that have been enunciated so far, even though he's been in office only a short time.

Some people might say, "Well, what do you expect?"

And the answer is that we expect a lot.

People say, "What, are you a dreamer?"

And the answer is, yes, we're dreamers. We want it all. We want a peaceful world. We want an egalitarian world. We don't want war. We don't want capitalism. We want a decent society.

We better hold on to that dream—because if we

don't, we'll sink closer and closer to this reality that we have, and that we don't want.

Be wary when you hear about the glories of the market system. The market system is what we've had. Let the market decide, they say. The government mustn't give people free health care; let the market decide. Which is what the market has been doing—and that's why we have forty-eight million people without health care. The market has decided that. Leave things to the market, and there are two million people homeless. Leave things to the market, and there are millions and millions of people who can't pay their rent. Leave things to the market, and there are thirty-five million people who go hungry.

You can't leave it to the market. If you're facing an economic crisis like we're facing now, you can't do what was done in the past. You can't pour money into the upper levels of the country—and into the banks and corporations—and hope that it somehow trickles down.

What was one of the first things that happened when the Bush administration saw that the economy was in trouble? A $700 billion bailout, and who did we give the $700 billion to? To the financial institutions that caused this crisis.

This was when the presidential campaign was still going on, and it pained me to see Obama standing there, endorsing this huge bailout to the corporations.

What Obama should have been saying was: Hey, wait a while. The banks aren't poverty-stricken. The CEOs aren't poverty-stricken. But there are people who are out of work. There are people who can't pay their mortgages. Let's take $700 billion and give it directly to the people who need it. Let's take $1 trillion, let's take $2 trillion.

Let's take this money and give it directly to the people who need it. Give it to the people who have to pay their mortgages. Nobody should be evicted. Nobody should be left with their belongings out on the street.

Obama wants to spend perhaps a trillion more on the banks. Like Bush, he's not giving it directly to homeowners. Unlike the Republicans, Obama also wants to spend $800 billion for his economic stimulus plan. Which is good—the idea of a stimulus is good. But if you look closely at the plan, too much of it goes through the market, through corporations.

It gives tax breaks to businesses, hoping that they'll hire people. No—if people need jobs, you don't give money to the corporations, hoping that maybe jobs will be created. You give people work immediately.

A lot of people don't know the history of the New Deal of the 1930s. The New Deal didn't go far enough, but it had some very good ideas. And the reason the New Deal came to these good ideas was because there was huge agitation in this country, and Roosevelt had to react. So what did he do? He took billions of dollars and said the government was going to hire people. You're out of work? The government has a job for you. As a result of this, lots of very wonderful work was done all over the country. Several million young people were put into the Civilian Conservation Corps. They went around the country, building bridges and roads and playgrounds, and doing remarkable things.

The government created a federal arts program. It wasn't going to wait for the markets to decide that. The government set up a program and hired thousands of unemployed artists: playwrights, actors, musicians, painters, sculptors, writers. What was the result? The result was the production of 200,000 pieces of art. Today, around the country, there are thousands of murals painted by people in the WPA program. Plays were put on all over the country at very cheap prices, so that people who had never seen a play in their lives were able to afford to go.

And that's just a glimmer of what could be done. The government has to represent the people's needs. The government can't give the job of representing the people's needs to corporations and the banks, because they don't care about the people's needs. They only care about profit.

In the course of his campaign, Obama said something that struck me as very wise—and when people say something very wise, you have to remember it, because they may not hold to it. You may have to remind them of that wise thing they said. Obama was talking about the war in Iraq, and he said, "It's not just that we have to get out of Iraq." He said "get out of Iraq," and we mustn't forget it. We must keep reminding him: Out of Iraq, out of Iraq, out of Iraq—not next year, not two years from now, but out of Iraq now.

But listen to the second part, too. His whole sentence was: "It's not enough to get out of Iraq; we have to get out of the mindset that led us into Iraq."

What is the mindset that got us into Iraq?

It's the mindset that says force will do the trick. Violence, war, bombers—that they will bring democracy and liberty to the people.

It's the mindset that says America has some God-given right to invade other countries for their own benefit. We will bring civilization to the Mexicans in 1846.

We will bring freedom to the Cubans in 1898. We will bring democracy to the Filipinos in 1900. You know how successful we've been at bringing democracy all over the world.

Obama has not gotten out of this militaristic missionary mindset. He talks about sending tens of thousands of more troops to Afghanistan.

Obama is a very smart guy, and surely he must know some of the history. You don't have to know a lot to know the history of Afghanistan has been decades and decades and decades and decades of Western powers trying to impose their will on Afghanistan by force: the English, the Russians, and now the Americans. What has been the result? The result has been a ruined country.

This is the mindset that sends 21,000 more troops to Afghanistan, and that says, as Obama has, that we've got to have a bigger military. My heart sank when Obama said that. Why do we need a bigger military? We have an enormous military budget. Has Obama talked about cutting the military budget in half or some fraction? No.

We have military bases in more than a hundred countries. We have fourteen military bases on Okinawa alone. Who wants us there? The governments. They get benefits. But the people don't really want us there. There have been huge demonstrations in Italy against the establishment of a U.S. military base. There have been big demonstrations in South Korea and on Okinawa.

One of the first acts of the Obama administration was to send Predator missiles to bomb Pakistan. People died. The claim is, "Oh, we're very precise with our weapons. We have the latest equipment. We can target anywhere and hit just what we want."

This is the mindset of technological infatuation. Yes, they can actually decide that they're going to bomb this one house. But there's one problem: They don't know who's in the house. They can hit one car with a rocket from a great distance. Do they know who's in the car? No.

And later—after the bodies have been taken out of the car, after the bodies have been taken out of the house—they tell you, "Well, there were three suspected terrorists in that house, and yes, there's seven other people killed, including two children, but we got the suspected terrorists."

But notice that the word is "suspected." The truth is they don't know who the terrorists are.

So, yes, we have to get out of the mindset that got us into Iraq, but we've got to identify that mindset. And Obama has to be pulled by the people who elected him, by the people who are enthusiastic about him, to renounce that mindset. We're the ones who have to tell him, "No, you're on the wrong course with this militaristic idea of using force to accomplish things in the world. We won't accomplish anything that way, and we'll remain a hated country in the world."

Obama has talked about a vision for this country. You have to have a vision, and now I want to tell Obama what his vision should be. The vision should be of a nation that becomes liked all over the world. I won't even say loved—it'll take a while to build up to that. A nation that is not feared, not disliked, not hated, as too often we are, but a nation that is looked upon as peaceful, because we've withdrawn our military bases from all these countries.

We don't need to spend the hundreds of billions of dollars on the military budget. Take all the money allocated to military bases and the military budget, and—this is part of the emancipation—you can use that money to give everybody free health care, to guarantee jobs to everybody who doesn't have a job, guaranteed payment of rent to everybody who can't pay their rent, build child care centers.

Let's use the money to help other people around the world, not to send bombers over there. When disasters take place, they need helicopters to transport people out of the floods and out of devastated areas. They need helicopters to save people's lives, and the helicopters are over in the Middle East, bombing and strafing people.

What's required is a total turnaround. We want a country that uses its resources, its wealth, and its power to help people, not to hurt them. That's what we need.

This is a vision we have to keep alive. We shouldn't be easily satisfied and say, "Oh, well, give him a break. Obama deserves respect."

But you don't respect somebody when you give them a blank check. You respect somebody when you treat them as an equal to you, and as somebody you can talk to and somebody who will listen to you.

Not only is Obama a politician. Worse, he's surrounded by politicians. And some of them he picked himself. He picked Hillary Clinton, he picked Lawrence Summers, he picked people who show no sign of breaking from the past.

We are citizens. We must not put ourselves in the position of looking at the world from their eyes and say, "Well, we have to compromise, we have to do this for political reasons." No, we have to speak our minds.

This is the position that the abolitionists were in

before the Civil War, and people said, "Well, you have to look at it from Lincoln's point of view." Lincoln didn't believe that his first priority was abolishing slavery. But the anti-slavery movement did, and the abolitionists said, "We're not going to put ourselves in Lincoln's position. We are going to express our own position, and we are going to express it so powerfully that Lincoln will have to listen to us."

And the anti-slavery movement grew large enough and powerful enough that Lincoln had to listen. That's how we got the Emancipation Proclamation and the Thirteenth and Fourteenth and Fifteenth Amendments.

That's been the story of this country. Where progress has been made, wherever any kind of injustice has been overturned, it's been because people acted as citizens, and not as politicians. They didn't just moan. They worked, they acted, they organized, they rioted if necessary to bring their situation to the attention of people in power. And that's what we have to do today.

INDEX

"Passim" (literally "scattered") indicates intermittent discussion of a topic over a cluster of pages.

books and reading, 37, 45, 76.
    See also novels; plays; poetry;
    textbook omissions
The Boondocks (comic strip), 109
Bork, Robert, 36
Boston University, 15–26
    passim, 45
boycotts, 46
Bradley, Bill, 69
Branch Davidian massacre,
    1993. *See* Waco siege, 1993
Brandon, William, 44
Bremer, Paul, 122, 123
Britain. *See* Great Britain
Brooks, David, 149
BU Exposure, 19–20
BU Five case, 22–24
BU News, 19
Bush, George H. W., 96, 116,
    181
Bush, George W., 69, 87–88,
    110–17 passim, 124, 127,
    205, 210–11; David Brooks
    in agreement with, 149;
    flip-flops on "success" in
    Iraq, 154; impeachment
    of (proposed), 107–8, 117,
    186–89 passim; John Kerry
    competition, 151, 155;
    reelection and second term,
    159–60, 165–69 passim;
    struts impotently, 179
Bush, Laura, 106–7, 108
business schools, 26

campaign speeches, 129–37
campus newspapers. *See* student
    newspapers
Canada, 222
capitalism, 34, 90, 201, 207, 230
Castro, Fidel, 71

Catch-22 (Heller), 81, 198
Cat's Cradle (Vonnegut), 199–200
Catonsville Nine case, 144
censorship, 19
Central Intelligence Agency.
    See CIA
Central Washington State
    University, 26
change of mind. *See* mind
    changing
Chechnya, 71–72, 155
chemical weapons, 132
Cheney, Dick, 10, 107, 111,
    186, 189
Cher, 133
children, Russian. *See* Russian
    children
children and war, 49, 71, 102,
    114; Afghan War, 97, 211;
    Gulf War, 53, 96; Iraq War,
    93, 110, 111, 115, 147, 154,
    162–67 passim; Korean War,
    209; Spanish-American War,
    113; Vietnam War, 31, 65,
    93, 95, 168, 209; Yugoslav
    Wars, 61–65 passim. *See also*
    infants and war
31, 65, 93, 95
Chomsky, Noam, 23, 45
Christianity, 200
CIA, 107, 163
CISPES. *See* Committee in
    Solidarity with the People of
    El Salvador (CISPES)
citizen-politician distinction,
    192, 195, 229, 236, 237
civil disobedience, 109–10,
    144–45, 163, 167, 188. *See
    also* sit-ins
Civilian Conservation Corps,
    232

Haiti, 113, 148, 216
Halliburton, 121, 164
Hapgood, Powers, 200
health insurance, universal. *See*
universal health insurance
Heller, Joseph, 198; *Catch-22*,
81, 198
Hersey, John: *The War Lover*,
179
Hezbollah, 180
higher education. *See*
universities and colleges
Hiroshima atomic bombing,
1945, 49, 55, 62–63, 142–43,
149, 175, 198, 227
historiography, 37, 44–45
history: study and teaching,
44–45
Hofstadter, Richard: *The
American Political Tradition*,
230
Holmes, Oliver Wendell, 140
Holocaust, Jewish. *See* Jewish
Holocaust
homelessness, 56, 207, 231
home loan foreclosures.
See mortgage loans and
foreclosures
Hoover, Herbert, 205, 206
House Committee on Un-
American Activities
(HUAC), 29, 30
Hughes, Langston, 81
hunger, 89–90, 231
Huntington, Samuel, 14
Hurricane Mitch, 55
Hussein, Saddam, 54, 70, 100,
108, 125, 136, 192, 210;
CIA opinion, 107; Iraqi
public opinion, 53, 115, 135;

United Nations and, 99
Hutto, Charles, 31, 32
hypocrisy, 55, 58, 84, 91, 98,
177, 198

immigrants, undocumented. *See*
undocumented immigrants
impeachment, 107–8, 117,
185–89 passim
imperialism, 111–13 passim,
117, 151, 163, 175
Indians. *See* Native Americans
Industrial Workers of the
World (IWW), 141, 142
inequality, 50, 223
infants and war, 61, 105, 162
internationalism, 48–49, 170–71
Iran, 87, 134
Iraq, 53–56, 62, 70, 72, 87,
93–102 passim, 153; Islamic
radicalization and, 157; U.S.
occupation, 115, 121–27
passim, 135, 147–51, 162–65
passim, 173, 179, 191–95
passim, 209–13 passim, 233.
See also Fallujah, Iraq; Gulf
War; Iraq War
Iraq War, 111–19 passim,
126–27, 130, 173, 177–79
passim, 185, 192, 195; costs,
131, 151; Iraqi death toll,
163, 182, 192; Obama policy,
217, 219, 233; presidential
candidates and, 206, 209–13
passim; run-up to, 103–9;
U.S. casualties, 133–34;
Vonnegut and, 198
Ireland, 193
Islamic radicalization, 157
Israel, 100, 108, 153–57 passim,

Mayer, Milton, 143
McCain, John, 69, 209–12
    passim
McFarlane, Robert, 30
McGruder, Aaron, 109
means and ends. *See* ends and
    means
media, 100, 104, 105, 154,
    161–62, 166, 169, 204. *See
    also* press; radio; television
medical insurance, universal. *See*
    universal health insurance
Mexicans: border crossing,
    123–24
military bases, 234, 235–36
military draft, 140, 141, 174,
    225–26
military occupations, 170; Iraq,
    115, 121–27, 135, 147–51,
    162–65 passim, 173, 179,
    191–95 passim, 209–13
    passim, 233; Palestine, 157
military operation naming, 112
military recruitment, 17, 25
military spending, 36, 51, 73,
    89, 114, 118, 130, 170,
    235–36; Iraq War, 131, 151;
    justification, 82; Obama
    and, 219, 234; presidential
    candidates and, 207; public
    opinion, 14, 36
Millay, Edna St. Vincent, 79–80
Milosevic, Slobodan, 57, 61,
    66, 67
missiles, cruise. *See* cruise
    missiles
missiles, Predator. *See* Predator
    missiles
Mississippi Freedom
    Democratic Party, 194

mind changing, 166, 167
Mr. Lif, 109
Moore, Michael, 118
mortgage loans and
    foreclosures, 203–4, 207, 231
Moscow purge trials, 75–76
MOVE bombing, Philadelphia,
    1985, 62
MoveOn, 191, 194
movies. *See* films
music, 85. *See also* songs
mutinies, 208, 224–25
My Lai massacre, 1968, 31, 32,
    61, 105, 162, 168

Nagasaki atomic bombing,
    1945, 55, 62–63, 142–43,
    175, 198, 227
naming of military operations.
    See military operation
    naming
national health insurance. *See*
    universal health insurance
nationalism, 114, 230
National Labor Relations Board
    (NLRB), 18
national security, 130–31
Native Americans, 44–45, 113,
    148, 169, 223
NATO, 59, 64–66 passim, 124,
    150
Nazis, 201–2, 228
neutrality, 40
New Deal, 206, 232–33
Newman, Richard, 19
newspapers, student. *See* student
    newspapers
New York City, 38–39
New York Times, 141, 198
Nicaragua, 30–31, 32

U.S. Constitution, 59, 186, 224, 237; impeachment and, 107, 117, 189; Patriot Act and, 124
U.S. Marine Corps, 16, 17
USSR. *See* Soviet Union
U.S. Supreme Court, 36, 55, 140–41

values, 48
Vanzetti, Bartolo, 200
Velde, Harold, 30
veterans' benefits, 131
veterans' demonstrations and actions, 206, 207
Vidanovic, Djordje, 63
"Vietnam syndrome," 96, 177, 181
Vietnam: The Logic of Withdrawal (Zinn), 129
Vietnam War, 55–61 passim, 82, 93–96 passim, 104–7 passim, 116, 126, 148, 176–77; African American opinion, 143–44; anticommunism and, 31, 32; Boston University role, 16; changing public opinion, 105, 116, 127, 162, 168, 176, 177; children and, 31, 65, 93, 95, 168, 209; Henry Kissinger and, 217; John Kerry fails to learn from, 150; Kurt Vonnegut and, 198; LBJ and, 129, 218–19; media coverage, 162; *Progressive* on, 143; U.S. bombing, 31, 55, 95, 168, 180; U.S. casualties, 95, 177, 209–10; Vietnamese casualties, 95, 182–83, 209
Vonnegut, Kurt, 81–82, 197–202

voting, 204–8 passim

Waco siege, 1993, 62
The War Lover (Hersey), 179
war, 173–83, 199, 228; direct action and, 208. *See also* children and war
"war on drugs," 181
"war on terrorism," 87–92, 124, 153–57, 163, 169, 177, 181–83 passim, 210–11
war resisters, 80, 82, 140, 141, 197
wars. *See* Civil War; Gulf War; Iraq War; Korean War; Revolutionary War; Spanish-American War; Vietnam War; World War I; World War II
Washington, George, 225
water privatization, 91
wealth gap. *See* inequality
"weapons of mass destruction," 55, 87, 99–100, 108; actually in the United States, 54, 97, 115–16, 132; allegedly in Iraq, 54, 87, 115, 134. *See also* chemical weapons; nuclear weapons
whistleblowers, 163
Wilson, Woodrow, 174, 216
The Wind That Shakes the Barley, 193
Wobblies. *See* Industrial Workers of the World (IWW)
Wolfowitz, Paul, 123
words, coined. *See* coined words
World War I, 139–42, 174–75, 216; civilian deaths, 101; e. e. cummings and, 80; in fiction,

ABOUT THE AUTHORS

Matthew Rothschild is the editor and publisher of the *Progressive* magazine, where he has worked since 1983. He's been editor since 1994. Rothschild is the author of *You Have No Rights: Stories of America in an Age of Repression* (New Press, 2007). He is the editor of *Democracy in Print: The Best of the Progressive, 1909–2009* (University of Wisconsin Press, 2009).

Howard Zinn (August 24, 1922–January 27, 2010) grew up in the immigrant slums of Brooklyn, where he worked in shipyards in his late teens. He saw combat duty as an air force bombardier in World War II and afterward received his doctorate in history from Columbia University and was a postdoctoral Fellow in East Asian Studies at Harvard University. Zinn is the author of many books, including his million-selling classic, *A People's History of the United States*, and *A Power Governments Cannot Suppress*.

Open Media is a movement-oriented publishing project committed to the vision of "one world in which many worlds fit"—a world with social justice, democracy, and human rights for all people. Founded in 1991 by Greg Ruggiero, Open Media has a history of producing critically acclaimed and best-selling titles that address the most urgent political and social issues of our time.

City Lights Open Media Series
www.citylights.com/collections/openmedia/